Unholy Mess

What the Bible Says About Clutter

Angie Hyche, CPO®

Shipshape Solutions

Kingsport

Shipshape Solutions
1657 E. Stone Dr., Suite B, #175
Kingsport, TN 37660

ISBN-10: 1-7349597-9-7

ISBN-13: 978-1-7349597-9-6

Library of Congress Control Number: 2020921780

Table of Contents

ꕤ

Introduction

We live in a culture of abundance. Most of us have the financial means to obtain every possession we need and much more. We have a full selection of activities from which to choose. We own devices that can help us find information, be entertained, and stay connected to friends and family at all times. But our abundance is both a blessing and a curse. We have filled our homes and our lives to overflowing. We have lost sight of what truly matters while chasing an ever-elusive sense of contentment.

As Christians, we were meant to live for much more than the shallow existence for which we have settled. Our Father longs for us to find our joy in our relationship with Him, not from what we buy or what we do.

This book will help you take an honest and objective look at your possessions and your activities. You'll find practical tools and tips to help you live an uncluttered life and to restore order and organization to your home and your schedule. You'll also find Scripture to inspire and encourage you along the way. Join me as we discover how to have a healthy relationship with our belongings and to experience the joy of an abundant life through Christ.

*Note: All client names contained in this book have been changed to protect their anonymity.

∞ 1 ∞

What Is Clutter?

When you hear the word "clutter," what comes to mind? Depending on how you view clutter, you may or may not think you have a problem with it. The real definition of clutter is so much more extensive and profound than what most people think. We need to make sure we're on the same page with a working definition.

When most people hear the word clutter, they usually picture a messy pile of stuff, a bunch of items in some sort of a less than ideal state. As far as definitions go, that's a good start, but we need to go much deeper. While clutter involving physical objects is the most recognized form, clutter includes so much more than just our stuff.

More broadly speaking, clutter is anything that gets in the way of what we want and need to do. It's anything that doesn't contribute to our best life or to reaching our goals. Clutter could include a list as diverse as this one: unused craft supplies, excess weight, outdated computer equipment, a hectic schedule, or a self-absorbed friend. Clutter draws our focus away from our true priorities. When we consider clutter in this broader sense, we can begin to see its pervasive effects. We can appreciate the fact that clutter includes so much more than physical objects. Our schedules and our minds can become cluttered as well.

I talk about clutter every day with my clients. My goal in our conversations is always to help them sharpen their focus so they see clearly what is important and what isn't. Whether we're discussing the condition of their bathroom vanity or of their calendar, the same principles apply. I want them to understand the only things that truly "belong" are the things they need to accomplish their purpose.

> Clutter is anything that doesn't contribute to our best life.

The following are examples to illustrate different types of clutter:

Brenda has lived in her home for over 30 years. She knows it's time for a downsize, but she's got a lot of work to do to get the home ready. She can't physically do all of the work herself, so she hired me to help. Brenda's goal is to prepare for an estate sale and then to sell the home.

A tour of the home reveals rooms crowded with stuff. Surfaces of furniture and portions of the floor are covered with items. One particularly crowded area is the master bathroom. Toiletries, medication, makeup, and jewelry obscure the surfaces.

We begin sorting through containers in the bedroom. If we find an item that already has a specific place where it belongs, Brenda tells me where to take it. However, every time I open a drawer or cabinet to place it there, there's no room; they're all full.

When we find books, she instructs me to move them to another room or to add them to other piles of books to sort later. She can't envision letting go of books because she loves them so much.

Piles of books and craft supplies line the hallway. Because of her health issues, she requires the assistance of a cane. The clutter is literally getting in her way because it blocks the hallway between the kitchen and the bedroom. But the clutter is also getting in her way figuratively. By choosing to shift most of the clutter to another location instead of letting it go, she isn't making much progress. I remind her that her new, smaller home will have even less space, but Brenda is still hesitant to part with much. Her physical clutter is most definitely getting in the way of her goal of getting her home ready to sell.

Andrea's story illustrates a different type of clutter. Andrea is a wife and mother of several children and works part-time. She is a very active volunteer in the community, and she loves to travel and entertain. As a driven extrovert, she loves the busy schedule, but the stress of planning and executing all of the events sometimes takes its toll. Because she's known for the excellent quality of her volunteer work, whether it's being neighborhood HOA President, homeroom mother, or soccer coach, she is frequently asked to volunteer more. She hates to say no, especially if it would leave someone else in a difficult situation. She usually agrees, and the frenetic pace continues.

It's very difficult for Andrea to step back and look objectively at the pace of her life. She knows she needs to have more free time so she doesn't feel like she's constantly playing catch up at home. It doesn't feel right to call the volunteer activities in which she participates "clutter." They are all good pursuits and noble uses of time, and she enjoys them all. But sometimes she gives so much time to others that she loses sight of one of her primary goals—to create a warm and peaceful space for herself, her husband, and her children. She can't live her best life if she's exhausted. Andrea's schedule clutter is getting in the way of her goals.

Jessie is a small business owner who is fiercely dedicated to her clients and to expanding her business. She works very hard to pivot her business with the changing times. She frequently launches new services to appeal to a different target market. She has so many more ideas she'd like to try that she has trouble focusing on just one thing at a time. At home when she's spending time with her husband and children, time and again she realizes that her mind has drifted back to work tasks. For example, she may miss half of the dinner conversation because she can't keep her mind focused on the present moment. Her family is frustrated with her lack of attention.

Coming face to face with your clutter can be truly life-changing. One Saturday in 2008, Joshua Becker began the dreaded project of cleaning the garage. His five-year-old son Salem asked him to play, and Joshua reluctantly explained that he needed to work. As the afternoon dragged on, Joshua became more and more frustrated to be spending his time decluttering the garage instead of playing

> Coming face to face with your clutter can be life-changing.

with his son. Clearly, his clutter was getting in his way.

Soon, a neighbor stopped by to chat. The neighbor had just had a conversation with her minimalist daughter, who told her mother she "didn't need to own all this stuff." When Becker relayed this conversation to his wife, the two of them made some major decisions. Not only did they decide to live a more intentional life and shed many of their belongings, but Becker changed his whole life's work to help others embrace the same transformation. He is now one of the world's foremost authorities on the minimalist lifestyle and the author of 4 bestselling books (including one of my favorites, *The More of Less*[1]).

As we discuss the many facets of clutter, you may see yourself in one or more of them. We're going to be taking a deep dive into different aspects of our lives. We'll examine our homes and our hearts against the standards of God's Word. This is not a journey for the faint of heart. My intention certainly isn't to make you feel guilty, although you will probably feel the sting of regret on some points. My goal is to inspire you to let go of the clutter so that you can embrace the abundant life God has promised you.

God has called us to a purposeful, fulfilling, and abundant life. He has a unique role for each one of us in His kingdom. He wants us to be so content and reassured of our identity in Him that we can't help but glorify Him with our lives. Our clutter, be it physical, spiritual, or mental, is robbing us of the peace and joy that could be ours. My earnest prayer is that the message of my book will help you experience the contentment that comes from the clutter-free and abundant life God intends for you.

∞ 2 ∞

How Does Our Clutter Affect Us?

O ur clutter affects us in innumerable ways, some more obvious than others. No one would be surprised to learn that clutter causes us to waste time. But did you know there is a link between excess weight and clutter? Have you ever thought household clutter could affect a school child's academic progress? How about a link between clutter and the risk of fire? You may find some of clutter's consequences startling. The more we learn about the far-reaching, deleterious effects of clutter, the more incentive we will have for change.

Feeling Overwhelmed

"I'm so overwhelmed!" It's a phrase I hear often. In fact, feeling overwhelmed is the top reason people contact me to get organizing help. The link between clutter and feeling overwhelmed is almost universal among my clients. When we're surrounded by clutter, everywhere we look, we see a visual reminder of what we need to do. It's very difficult to relax in a cluttered environment. We may be able to ignore it for a while, but eventually the feeling of being overwhelmed will eat away at us so much that we'll be compelled to either give up or to finally take action.

Wasted Time and Money

Losing things is perhaps one of life's greatest frustrations. Think about the countless times you've lost your keys, purse, wallet, remote, cell phone, one earring of a pair, umbrella, password, gift card, etc. Need I go on? We're exasperated, and we may feel like we're losing our minds. It's even worse when we have made a special effort to put something in a particular place because it made such logical sense for it to be there. The connection was so rational at the time that we were convinced we would remember it. When we don't, we're angry at ourselves, and we feel a lack of control and helplessness.

Have you ever considered how much our clutter contributes to this tendency? Of course, there are many other factors contributing to losing things (such as forgetfulness, stress, fatigue, some medical issues, etc.). Still, clutter plays a huge role. When items don't have established homes (or they aren't returned to their established homes after use), surfaces become covered with items, and items are then piled in random places. It's no wonder we struggle. Throw in a cluttered schedule and a cluttered mind, and you've got the perfect storm for losing things.

The statistics on lost items always amaze me, but they don't really surprise me. Take a look at these survey results from an October 2016 Lost and Found study:[2]

- Americans spend 2.5 days a year looking for lost items.

- Every year, over $2.7 billion is spent replacing misplaced possessions.

- People suffer other consequences of losing items:

  - 60% of survey respondents have been late for work or school.

  - 49% have missed an important appointment or meeting.

  - 35% have argued with a significant other.

  - 22% have missed a plane, train, or bus.

There is an entire burgeoning industry centered around technology to help us recover missing items. Companies like Tile, TrackR, Click 'n Dig, Whistle, and Orbit specialize in devices and technology to help us find lost items. Whether it's a remote, keys, wallet, eyeglasses, a parked car, or your pet, there is some kind of tech solution to help you. A quick online search will help you find currently ranked apps, products, and companies.

The simple fact that an entire industry has developed for the specific purpose of finding lost items is evidence of the prevalence of the problem. It stands to reason that the more items we own, the more likely we are to misplace some of those items.

Depression and Stress

Depression is a pervasive disorder in our current culture. Because there is such a vast array of contributing factors, it's not always easy to tease out individual factors. That being said, based on my experience as an organizer, clutter definitely correlates with depression. While this fact may seem, well, depressing, the positive side is that fixing our clutter problems can be one part of the remedy.

In a 2009 study of dual-income, middle-class families in a large U.S. city, 30 couples gave tours of their homes and recorded the tours via camcorder. Scientists used reports of mood and levels of the hormone cortisol to study the participants' stress levels. The study found that women who described their home with terms such as "messy, cluttered, disarrayed, unorganized, disorganized, overflowing, chaotic, haphazard, unfinished, half-finished or sloppy" showed evidence of a depressed mood and chronic stress.[3]

Since this study finding describes the effect on women, perhaps you're wondering if clutter has a similar effect on men. In short, the answer is no. Husbands in this study didn't experience the same stress with a messy house, and their mood didn't improve with a more restful home. The authors postulated that women may be more sensitive to their home environment and/or may feel a greater responsibility for the state of the home.

Overeating and Excess Weight

When clutter is everywhere in the home, it's hard to get motivated to do anything, and healthy eating habits require motivation. It's tempting to look around at a cluttered environment and think, "Well, I can't take care of my home. Why should I even try to take care of myself? I'm just going to eat because it feels good." One bad habit leads to another and another. It all gets to be too much. Too much stuff, too much work to change, too much to eat. We can get stuck in a self-perpetuating vicious cycle.

In a study reported in a February 2016 NPR article "A Cluttered Kitchen Can Nudge Us to Overeat,"[4] participants were placed in either a room cluttered with papers and office supplies or in a clutter-free room and were given a choice of snacks. Participants in the clutter-free room were more likely to choose healthy snacks.

A study aimed at the effects of clutter and hoarding showed that hoarding participants were three times more likely to be overweight or obese than were family members. Hoarding participants were also significantly more likely to report a broad range of chronic and severe medical concerns and had a fivefold higher rate of mental health service utilization.[5]

Both of the above studies provide some evidence of the correlation between clutter and a tendency towards overeating and excess weight. I'm not surprised by the connection. In fact, many of these factors are interdependent. For example, we've already discussed the relationship between clutter and depression. Since depression is also associated with overeating and excess weight, it makes sense that clutter would be associated with excess weight as well.

If clutter is correlated with overeating and weight gain, could the opposite also be true? Could decluttering correlate with weight loss? After helping people with clutter for over 13 years, organizing expert Peter Walsh had anecdotally observed that one of the biggest benefits people had gained after dealing with their clutter was weight loss. It was such a powerful trend that Walsh developed a six-week program and set up a test panel of 25 people with both clutter and weight issues. The findings were encouraging. The average weight loss was 10 pounds.[6]

Embarrassment and Isolation

By nature, we want to present ourselves in the most positive light. Right or wrong, our homes can sometimes feel like an extension of ourselves. When our homes are cluttered, we are often understandably hesitant to invite others into them. Taken to an extreme, this can lead to isolation.

One of my very first clients hadn't been able to entertain guests in her home for years. As an extrovert and a family-oriented person, this greatly troubled her. Her goal for our organizing sessions was to finally feel comfortable inviting extended family members to stay with them over the holidays. I was thrilled when she contacted me after the holidays to tell me how much they had enjoyed having holiday guests again.

Embarrassment can stop people from calling me in the first place. Even when someone does call, they sometimes choose not to proceed. I have encountered this embarrassment so frequently that I have almost come to expect it.

Difficulty with Focus

When our environment is cluttered with stuff, it's no wonder we have trouble focusing. My clients call me because they can't seem to stay focused while working through a room full of clutter. Even I sometimes have a hard time focusing on one object in the midst of many. Research confirms that our brains have trouble blocking out clutter.

In a June 2015 issue of *Princeton Alumni Weekly*, Michael Blanding explains the findings of research by

Princeton neuroscientist and professor Sabine Kastner. "In any environment," she concluded, "there is both a 'push' toward desired objects and a 'pull' from objects competing for attention. The more objects in the visual field, the harder the brain has to work to filter them out, causing it to tire over time and reducing its ability to function."[7]

Home Isn't Quite as Homey

Most of us would agree with Dorothy's sentiment in *The Wizard of Oz*, "there's no place like home." However, if your home is cluttered, you probably won't feel those emotions as strongly. According to research reported in the June 2016 issue of the *Journal of Experimental Psychology*, clutter prevents us from feeling comfortable and content in our home.[8] In other words, home doesn't feel as much like home when it's cluttered.

When home doesn't feel like home, you may feel stressed, overwhelmed, and so depressed that you're tempted to overeat. Your home isn't the peaceful refuge you want it to be. When we're not at peace, our emotions make us more likely to participate in unhealthy behaviors like overeating. The emotional aspects of the situation can feel like a vicious cycle.

Risking Our Children's Future

This particular effect of clutter is more complicated than just a simple case of children not learning organizational skills at home. The effects of a cluttered home contribute to deeper problems with a child's behavior and academic success. Studies in 2005 and 2011 of children raised in chaotic homes (defined by noise, overcrowding, and a lack of order) showed lower scores on tests of self-regulatory capabilities and cognitive ability, poorer language abilities, and more problem behaviors and learned helplessness than in children raised in less chaotic environments.[9]

Organizing is a skill that can be learned just like any other skill. By improving the order of your home, you can teach your children essential skills that will improve their academic

> ## Organizing is a skill that can be learned.

success and serve them throughout their lives.

Increased Risk of Falls

Falls are the leading cause of both fatal and non-fatal injuries for older Americans.[10] Clutter greatly increases the risk of falling or other injuries. I am a healthy, able-bodied woman without any physical limitations or issues with balance. I've had plenty of experience working in cluttered spaces and am aware that I need to use caution. Still, I've had my fair share of injuries while helping people clear clutter. With clutter on floors and a lack of clear, wide pathways in the home, slipping and falling are practically inevitable.

An increased risk of falls is especially true for segments of the population already at risk, such as people on medications with contributing side effects, people with underlying health issues, people with mobility issues, poor vision, or issues with balance. Most seniors fit into several of these categories. It stands to reason that clearing clutter, especially in the most commonly used pathways in a home (hallways to and from the garage, bedroom, living room, kitchen, and bathroom) can tremendously decrease the fall risk.

One of my client's parents has significant mobility issues, and my client was worried about the clutter in their home. In particular, their garage didn't have a clear path from the car to the house because of all of the accumulated clutter. Since her parents aren't physically able to do all of the work associated with decluttering, she has devoted many hours to assisting them. By alleviating some of their clutter, she has made their home a safer environment. I am so proud to see her pass along the decluttering skills she has learned in our organizing sessions to her parents.

Increased Fire Risk

Every home is susceptible to damage from a fire, but a cluttered home is even more susceptible. It's not too difficult to imagine that a home or office filled with clutter would pose many additional challenges in the event of a fire. The clutter will likely contain a large amount of combustible materials like trash, paper, and clothing which provide fuel for the fire. There is more risk of structural damage or building collapse because of the additional weight of the clutter. Emergency responders and residents of the home or office will have a more difficult time getting in or out of the building if doors, windows, and hallways are blocked by clutter.[11]

The list of clutter's effects is quite impressive. I wasn't even aware of some of these until I started doing research. And I certainly didn't know many of these effects had been studied. After reading this chapter, we can easily conclude that physical clutter has extensive negative effects.

We've really only scratched the surface when it comes to clutter's effects. If we want to confront the full scope of clutter, we need to dig a little deeper. While physical clutter is rampant in American society, there are many more types of clutter that we haven't explored. These clutter categories are more difficult to detect. Although often invisible to the naked eye, their consequences are just as dangerous, if not more so, than those we've already addressed.

The next chapter is a very personal look at two of the most serious and pervasive types of clutter today. While I've never had much of a problem with physical clutter, I am by no means immune to clutter and its effects. I am following the Biblical principle of looking at myself first before I judge others (Matthew 7:1–5). As it turns out, I am somewhat of an expert in the more hidden types of clutter. It's not something I'm proud of. I share humbly in hopes that you will learn from my mistakes.

ℬ 3 ℭ

What's My Clutter Story?

I n 2017, my husband Eric and I began preparing to downsize to a much smaller space. I bragged that we didn't have much clutter, so we probably wouldn't have too much stuff to donate. This preparation to downsize forced us to take a hard look at every single item we owned and to make some tough decisions. I wish I had weighed our donations. We certainly had much more clutter than either of us anticipated! We sold or donated a whole lot of items, but it wasn't too difficult overall. Of the hundreds of items we let go, I've only missed ten or so, and even then, I don't regret our choice.

The more I help people declutter, the more conscious I am of my own clutter and the more willing I am to let it go. It's a continual process. Like most everyone, I have a few categories in which I tend to overbuy; I have to really watch myself when it comes to purchases of home decor or clothes.

I may not struggle too much with physical clutter, but over the last few years I have realized I have a real problem with two other kinds of clutter: schedule and attention clutter. You may not think to call them "clutter." However, recall the broader definition of clutter from Chapter 1. Clutter is anything that gets in the way of what we want and need to do. It's anything that doesn't contribute to our best life or to reaching our goals. Clutter draws our focus away from our true priorities. From that standpoint, I can certainly label my issues as clutter.

Schedule Clutter

America is by and large a culture of the busy. A packed schedule is often viewed as a badge of honor. It's as if our importance is defined by the number of activities on our calendar. As an energetic extrovert, I've found a crowded calendar is addictive. In fact, I think a demanding schedule is slightly thrilling. Part of the issue is that I love a challenge, and a myriad of irons in the fire is nothing if not a challenge.

> America is a culture of the busy.

I have convinced myself time and time again that I thrive on this lifestyle. I am reminded of a scene in one of my very favorite books. In *Anne of Green Gables* by Lucy Maud Montgomery, neighbor Mrs. Lynde is in the process of telling the main character Anne Shirley that she's glad Anne has given up her notion of going to college. Anne explains she has no intention of giving up her studies. In light of Anne's adoptive mother Marilla's illness, Anne will continue her courses at home. This excerpt of the ensuing conversation is memorable:

> Mrs. Lynde lifted her hands in holy horror.
> 'Anne Shirley, you'll kill yourself.'
> 'Not a bit of it. I shall thrive on it...'[12]

In the midst of my bursting-at-the-seams schedule, I was convinced that, like Anne, I was indeed thriving. But the truth is that I was exhausted. I was trying to spin too many plates, not putting the most important things first, and neglecting my family. My life was incredibly out of balance.

I teach a time management and productivity class. At the beginning of the class, I show a beautiful photo of one of my favorite hikes in the Rocky Mountains. It's an idyllic image of a snow-capped mountain reflected in a lake, and across the bottom of the image is a quote: "The two most important days of your life are the day you are born and the day you figure out why." Then I talk about the importance of priorities, emphasizing that we have to keep a proper perspective, and that our priorities should be the most important factor in choosing how we spend our time. I hadn't even taken the time to consider my priorities, much less to use them as the basis for my decisions. I should have been listening to my own advice!

Upon further reflection, I am now convinced part of the reason I filled my schedule so full was to avoid figuring out my priorities. Answering those big life questions takes deep reflection. I never had time for reflection, and I didn't really want to make an effort to find the time, although I'm not sure I realized it. Besides, I prided myself on being a model of productivity. I was almost obsessed with checking off items on my long, ever-present To-Do list. I labored under the illusion that if I checked off enough items, I could relax. But like an eternal assembly line, as soon as I checked off one item, two or three would take its place.

After years of this pace and the anxiety it produced, at long last I realized I would have to change. For the good of myself and my family, I needed to take some drastic measures. Bible study, prayer, counseling, and the encouragement of friends and family were key components of my process.

Although I've changed drastically, if I don't pay enough attention, I can still easily get sucked right back into it. It is a continual process, not just a one-time event. Isn't that true of any big change in our habits? We have to keep revisiting the core issues and make adjustments if we want to continue to be successful. I'll share specific strategies I used to declutter my schedule in Chapter 11: "How Do I Declutter My Schedule and My Mind?".

Attention Clutter

I have a huge issue with what I choose to call attention clutter. Another name for this category is mental clutter. When I refer to attention clutter, I'm talking about the way our minds are constantly absent from the here and now. It's a lack of focus, a lack of ability to concentrate on the person or task at hand, not being "in the moment." Just like schedule clutter, this kind of clutter isn't visible to the eye. But its effects are extremely damaging. It causes us to do a poor job at whatever task we're trying to work on because our mind isn't there. It can be especially damaging to relationships because we treat others around us as if they aren't important.

Attention clutter has been manifested in my life in many forms. One prime example of my own attention clutter is my propensity for losing things. As I am now squarely in the thick of middle age, I'm told this tendency will only get worse. Heaven help my family.

To make matters worse, I don't just struggle with losing things at home. I leave items at client's houses on a semi-regular basis. In the spirit of true confession, I have left all of the following items at a client's home at least once: water bottle, portable table, label maker, organizing bag of supplies, cell phone, cleaning solution, and packing tape. In a crowning moment and all-time low, when my husband drove me to the airport for my first NAPO (National Association of Productivity and Organizing Professionals) conference, I didn't realize until we arrived at the airport that I had left my suitcase at home. I missed my flight and had to wait until the next morning to fly.

Thankfully, I still made it in time to enjoy all of the conference. It made for great table conversation at the conference. Talk about a cluttered mind, a cluttered schedule, and the resulting lack of attention to detail! As funny as some of these stories may be, my attention clutter is really no laughing matter. It has real consequences that draw my focus away from what really matters.

Another way in which attention clutter is displayed in my life is a general focus on myself to the exclusion of others. Left to my own devices, I tend to have an "all about me" kind of approach to life. I can easily get preoccupied with how something will affect me, what I need or deserve, why I wasn't included in something I thought I should have been, and any number of other egotistical thoughts. It's no wonder someone who is focused on themselves would have trouble paying attention to what's going on around them.

When we're busy ruminating on our own issues, it's almost impossible to be fully present in the moment.

Here's one example of my self-focus. I will often ask Eric a question, but before he even finishes answering it, my mind has jumped forward to a completely different topic (most commonly it's my beloved To-Do list). After he finishes answering the question, I have no idea what he just said.

Although there are other factors contributing to attention clutter, I want to concentrate on the contributor that has caused the most problems in my life in the last few years. It's probably the single factor causing unprecedented levels of attention clutter in our culture. Let me tell you about my addiction to my smartphone.

This truth is painful to admit. I have made much progress, but I still have a long way to go. The worst part of this realization is it took years for me to admit it and to actually make a change, even though my family had been telling me I had a problem. They told me that many times, when they were trying to talk to me, I was paying more attention to my phone than I was to them. I usually had an excuse (rarely a good excuse). I made half-hearted efforts to decrease my smartphone use. Change did not come easy. In the end, it took radical decisions to alter my patterns of behavior. I'll share the decisions and solutions in Chapter 11, "How Do I Declutter My Schedule and My Mind?".

I know I am not alone in this struggle. From the article "45 Scary Smartphone Addiction Statistics, 2019"[13], here are some alarming statistics about smartphone addiction:

- The average smartphone owner unlocks their phone 150 times a day.

- Users spend on average 2 hours and 51 minutes a day on their smartphones. In comparison, the quality time people spend with their families amounts to less than 45 minutes a day.

- 58% of smartphone users don't go 1 hour without checking their phones.

- The average user touches their phone 2,617 times a day.

- 71% usually sleep with or next to their mobile phones.

- 80% of smartphone users check their phone within 1 hour of waking or going to sleep.

- 75% of users admit that they have texted at least once while driving.

- 85% of smartphone users will check their device while speaking with friends and family.

- Adults spend on average 45 minutes per day on social media.

- We'll spend an average of 5 years and four months of our lifetimes on social media.

I don't know how those statistics make you feel, but I find them frightening and sobering. Before you say (or think), "I believe it! Teenagers these days are just so addicted to their phones," keep in mind these statistics include all ages, not just teenagers.

Before you say (or think), "Yeah, some people really do have a problem with their phones, but not me," take a look at yourself. Better yet, ask your close friends and family members whether it's an issue with you, and tell them you are ready to hear the truth. At the end of our lives, we may say, "I wish I had spent more time with my family and friends." I don't think anyone will ever say, *"I wish I had spent more time on my smartphone."*

Think about the days before we had smartphones. I know—it's hard to remember! If we wanted to get a message to someone, we had a few options. We could tell them in person (remember when drop-in visits weren't considered rude?), send a letter (aka snail-mail), or call them (on their landline). Then sometime in the '80s, cell phones gained in popularity, enabling us to reach someone away from home (a whole new exciting option!). Sometime in the '90s, email came along, offering yet another alternative. We still couldn't rely on quick responses to emails because we couldn't yet get emails on our phones.

Although smartphone development originated in the '90s, the true smartphone revolution began when Steve Jobs revealed the first iPhone in 2007. As the article "A Brief History of the Smartphone" describes it, that was "the day we lost our attention spans."[14] Consider the changes in communication ushered in with the widespread use of smartphones. Now we have all of the following options to stay in touch: in person visit (yeah, right), snail-mail (not likely), email (yay for instant access, but usually replies take too long), phone calls (in any location as long as there is a signal, which is almost everywhere), and now texting (which has become the preferred method for most people). Of course, there's also Facebook Messenger, GroupMe, Snapchat, WhatsApp, and so many more. All enable practically instant communication on our smartphones. Which we always have with us. Even when we sleep. Or try to sleep.

It's all a bit mind-boggling, isn't it? No doubt there are positive aspects of quick communication. In case of emergency, I am comforted that I *can* be reached instantly. In truth, messages occasionally need a hasty answer. But here's the rub: just because we can reply quickly doesn't mean we *need* to reply quickly. Just because we sent a question by text only requiring a brief answer doesn't mean the recipient needs to answer immediately or that we should be frustrated with the other person if they don't.

Our family has debated this matter extensively. We've had some great insights about how our expectations have changed over time. Whether consciously or not, we've set the expectation that messages of any kind should be answered quickly, even if they don't need to be. Our phones ring or beep or vibrate or play our favorite ringtone, and our instinctive impulse is to jump into action. We might be in the middle of an urgent work project or a weighty conversation with a loved one. We might be relaxing with a good book, hiking on a peaceful trail, or pondering the meaning of life. If we read that text, answer that phone call, check that email, or scan that Facebook message, the moment is lost. We're no longer "in the moment." Our train of thought is interrupted. If we're with others, whether we intended to or not, that simple action has communicated they aren't quite as valued as whatever we just checked on our phone.

I'm grateful I was finally made aware of the severity of my attention clutter so I could make changes. No, it's not perfect now, but it's much better.

The changes I've made with schedule and attention clutter have changed my personal life and my family life for the better in so many ways. The same could be true for you if you're willing to face up to and tackle unhealthy smartphone habits. You'll find tips for breaking bad habits with your smartphone in Chapter 11: "How Do I Declutter My Schedule and My Mind?".

Both schedule clutter and attention clutter are an ongoing struggle for me, and I have definitely not arrived. I share these details in hopes that you will be inspired and challenged if you also need to make a change. I pray God can use my mistakes to make a difference for you.

❧ 4 ☙

What Does the Bible Say About Clutter?

All of the consequences of clutter we have considered are significant, and avoiding the consequences can no doubt give us motivation for change. However, as Christians, our primary motivation should be a desire to glorify God, and our primary inspiration should be God's Word. We need to dive into the Scripture to see what the Bible has to say to guide us in our efforts to change.

In truth, the word "clutter" isn't in the Bible. I'm not even sure anyone in biblical times used a similar word. That being said, the Bible has plenty to say about clutter and about disorder. When we evaluate our lives to assess any issues we might have with clutter, our job is not just to examine our belongings and our time and whether they're organized (or not). The real crux of our evaluation should be in our attitudes and in our hearts. What do we consider most important? What are we prioritizing? What holds our attention? What do we think about and talk about most?

Our clutter is holding us back from the purposeful, fulfilling, and abundant life God has planned for us. My intention is to help you take an honest look at your life. How do you view your possessions, your time, and your money? Do you see all of them as gifts from God to be used for His glory? Is clutter in some form taking a toll on you?

We serve a God who is all-knowing and all-powerful, who created the world by speaking it into existence. Yet He knows and loves each one of us. He alone knows what's best for us, and He knows what will truly give us contentment and peace (and what won't). As sons and daughters of God, let's refuse to settle for less than what He intends for us. Let's reject the false promise of finding happiness in anything less than a life of glorifying and serving God.

> God knows what will give us contentment and peace and what won't.

The Scriptures in the following chapters are divided into four main topics: A God of Order, Spiritual Perspective, Godly Priorities, and God's Promises. For the most part, I will be using the New International Version (NIV) of the Bible. It's my preferred version in terms of readability and accuracy. Grab your Bible (physical or digital) and let's dig in!

ೞ 5 ೞ

A God of Order

We don't have to go very far in reading the Bible to find evidence that our God is a God of order. From the very first verses in the book of Genesis, we encounter God's detailed plan for bringing the universe into existence. Creation is the supreme example of an ordered process. God didn't just haphazardly speak everything into existence. He had a definite order and accomplished the monumental undertaking in calculated steps. When we look at individual parts of Creation, we see an awe-inspiring amount of order down to the tiniest detail. God's wisdom, power, intelligence, and creativity are in full display all around us.

> In the beginning God created the heavens and the earth. Now the earth was formless and empty, darkness was over the surface of the deep, and the Spirit of God was hovering over the waters. And God said, 'Let there be light,' and there was light. God saw that the light was good, and he separated the light from the darkness. God called the light 'day,' and the darkness he called 'night.' And there was evening, and there was morning—the first day.
>
> Genesis 1:1–5 (NIV)

Examples of God's emphasis on order can be found throughout the Bible. Consider the specifics of God's instructions for building the ark and the tabernacle. God had specific requirements for ceremonies and sacrifices. Order is a consistent biblical maxim.

The New Testament also contains examples of order. One such example is in I Corinthians 14, in which Paul is addressing a problem in the church in Corinth. Apparently, their worship services had become chaotic. Various people were singing, prophesying, speaking in tongues, and interpreting, sometimes all at the same time. The lack of order was keeping their worship from lifting up God effectively and from being beneficial for everyone. After giving suggestions for solving the specific problem, Paul writes this verse:

> For God is not a God of disorder but of peace.
>
> I Corinthians 14:33 (NIV)

If God is not a God of disorder, He is a God of order. In this passage, God is linked to order, and order is linked to peace. Peace and order go hand in hand in this Scripture. On a broader scale, peace and order go hand in hand in our lives.

When our home, our schedule, and our thoughts are in order, life is so much more peaceful. We can move around our home freely,

> **Peace and order go hand in hand in our lives.**

unencumbered by clutter. We can find what we need because everything is in the place where it belongs. We're able to relax and spend time doing what we enjoy with the people we love because our schedule isn't stuffed too full. Because we've prioritized the state of our soul and our mind, our minds are freed for creative and inspirational thoughts. When the mental clutter that clouds our minds and steals our focus is gone, our hearts, minds, and souls are at peace. We are more connected to the people around us, and more importantly, we are more connected to God.

❧ 6 ☙

Spiritual Perspective

Have you ever noticed that the ways of God frequently run completely counter to the ways of this world? When you compare what the world values and what God values, they are often complete opposites. This fact alone sometimes makes the Bible challenging to comprehend and difficult to put into practice. For example, from a worldly perspective, we all want to be first, and we are sometimes willing to do whatever it takes to win. From a spiritual perspective, Jesus said whoever wants to be first should be last (Matthew 20:26).

It would be an interesting experiment to watch people's reactions if we were to apply this perspective in everyday life. What if at the end of a race, we awarded a first-place trophy to the last runner to cross the finish line? People might think we're crazy!

I for one want to be sure I am placing things in the right perspective, the godly perspective. If I try to count on just doing what comes naturally, I'll fail most of the time. A godly perspective doesn't come naturally. It must be learned from God's Word and then practiced in our actions. Adopting a godly perspective requires a conscious decision. And it all starts with the precepts set out in the Scripture.

It's All from God

We have to begin a discussion of spiritual perspective by acknowledging God gave us everything good in our lives. But even more fundamental is the fact that we wouldn't even be here if not for God! Light and dark, plants and animals, waters, sky, sun and moon, and everything else in the universe was made by God. While every single part of the cosmos is impressive, God's crowning achievement, His most remarkable creation, His one achievement that stands far and away at the top all of them is us!

> So don't be misled, my dear brothers and sisters. Whatever is good and perfect is a gift coming down to us from God our Father...And we, out of all creation, became his prized possession.
>
> James 1:17–18 New Living Translation (NLT)

For this reference, I chose the New Living Translation because the vocabulary is much more recognizable. The NIV refers to us as "firstfruits," which is not a term in common use.

As Christians, we know (at least logically) everything we have comes from God. We can truthfully take no personal credit for one single element, be it a belonging, a talent, an idea, or a position. Even if we have worked hard in school or at our jobs to "earn" money or goods, we know our opportunities and abilities are God-given as well. In Psalms 89, the writer is speaking to God about the world that He created.

> The heavens are yours, and yours also the earth; you founded the world and all that is in it.
>
> Psalms 89:11 (NIV)

When we talk about the things we "own," we have to remember we really don't own them; God does. And even when we talk about our skills/talents/abilities, we have to remember that without God, we wouldn't have any of these. It is our nature to forget this fact. From the beginning of time, God's people had to be reminded of this time and time again. And so do we. It's kind of humbling, isn't it?

> You may say to yourself, 'My power and the strength of my hands have produced this wealth for me.' But remember the Lord your God, for it is he who gives you the ability to produce wealth, and so confirms his covenant."
>
> Deuteronomy 8:17–18 (NIV)

Without a doubt, everything good in our lives is from God. It may not have come wrapped up with a bow, but it's all a gift from God. He gave us everything we have! Along with our physical gifts are spiritual gifts of an infinitely greater value. These spiritual gifts put into perspective even more our place and our purpose in God's kingdom.

> For it is by grace you have been saved, through faith—and this is not from yourselves, it is the gift of God—not by works, so that no one can boast. For we are God's handiwork, created in Christ Jesus to do good works, which God prepared in advance for us to do.
>
> Ephesians 2:8–10 (NIV)

This has always been one of my favorite Bible verses. First of all, it points to the most wondrous of all our gifts from God—our salvation. We couldn't possibly do enough to earn it. This gift came with an unfathomable price tag; it required the blood of Jesus. God's only Son, the sinless Lamb of God, paid the price for your sin and my sin when He died on the cross.

We are described in this passage as "God's handiwork," and this passage says we were "created in Christ Jesus to do good works, which God prepared in advance for us to do." We are God's masterpiece, the result of His incredible power and creativity. He made us for the purpose of doing good works. We can certainly use our possessions for this purpose. Our excess, our clutter can be put to good use for others. We were made to serve and glorify God, and to live with Him for eternity. No wonder we aren't satisfied by our earthly lives; we have a much higher calling!

> No wonder we aren't satisfied by our earthly lives; we have a much higher calling!

Here's the part that gets me every time. We like to be noticed for the good things we do, but we can't even take credit for those good things! God set those situations up for us! He knew where we would live, what we would be like, and who we would meet. Let that sink in for a moment. God knew exactly when and where you would be born and every single detail of your life before you were even conceived. He knew where you would go to school, who would be your best friend in elementary school, what your personality would be like, whether you would have blue eyes or brown, and what your favorite color would be. He knew the trivial and the important. He gave you life and breath and everything else. God's greatest desire was for you to seek Him. He wants you to see His love and His power and His goodness, to know Him, to live for Him, and to share this abundant life with all who cross your path.

What Fills Us Up?

We have established through Scripture that God made us and everything else in all creation, and that everything we have was given to us by God. We have truly been blessed by so many good gifts, both physical and spiritual. Because God made us, He knew we would only find true happiness if we could see these gifts from the proper perspective. Ultimately, we were never meant to be happy with this earthly life anyway. First and foremost, God made us to be His children, to rely on Him as Our Father, to find meaning in Him and Him alone. We humans are constantly looking for happiness in the wrong things. This tendency began from the very first days of creation, with Adam and Eve looking for something more in the Garden of Eden, and it continues throughout all of time.

Perhaps the most comprehensive search for the true source of happiness is found in Ecclesiastes. King Solomon's quest for meaning was extensive. He tried to find meaning in a host of things, including wisdom and knowledge, pleasures of all kinds (wine, houses, vineyards, slaves, silver and gold, singers, and a harem), work, advancement in position, and wealth. Because he possessed immense wealth and power, he had the unique opportunity to exhaust every possible source of meaning.

Solomon tried it all. Each time he tried something new, Solomon concluded it didn't bring contentment. You can just hear his frustration in this passage:

> The words of the Teacher, son of David, king in Jerusalem: 'Meaningless! Meaningless!' says the Teacher. 'Utterly meaningless! Everything is meaningless.'
>
> Ecclesiastes 1:1–2 (NIV)

Solomon didn't find happiness in his stuff. And neither will we.

This is not earth-shattering news. We know our possessions don't bring us contentment. At least, we know this logically. Yet many of us keep trying this route. We may not even be aware we are using this strategy to find contentment. We may feel a small amount of temporary satisfaction with our purchases. So we keep going, fooling ourselves into thinking just a little more will quench our unending thirst. Advertisements fuel our drive to continue purchasing by showing us images of happy customers enjoying their purchases. We forget that the satisfaction after a purchase is temporary and that we have to find space amidst our clutter for those new items, then find time to maintain them.

Solomon didn't find happiness in his work, in wealth, in power, or in his relationships. Solomon had many wives and concubines. He had plenty of chances to test out the theory that "just one more relationship will make me happy." It didn't work for him, and it won't work for us either. He had all the earthly wealth he could ever want, but wealth didn't make him happy either. Solomon didn't find happiness in any of the countless things he tried. And neither will we. We spend so much time and effort in this exhausting search for meaning and for happiness. But we're looking in all of the wrong places.

I am reminded of a ladies Bible study I attended over 20 years ago while living in Atlanta. My friend Teresa was teaching, and her lesson has stuck with me after all these years. She held up her daughter's doll with a compartment in its back for batteries. I don't remember what the batteries enabled the doll to do, but for the purposes of the study, it didn't matter because there were no batteries in the compartment. She explained that the only item that could really fit into the compartment and allow the doll to operate to its full capability was the specific batteries it was designed to hold. Then she made the parallel to our lives. Just like the doll without batteries, each of us has a void in our lives, a hole we try to fill with countless things. Just as the doll's compartment can only be filled perfectly with the exact batteries it needs, the hole in us is God-shaped, and only God can fill it perfectly.

At this point in the study, Teresa pulled out more props. Each one represented something we try to fit into the void in our lives to make us happy. She tried stuffing each one into the doll's battery compartment, but of course none of them fit or made the doll work. She tried to fit small playhouse people into the compartment, representing relationships we think will make us happy (friends, husband, etc.). She tried putting play food into it, representing how we sometimes eat in an attempt to fill that void. She tried sticking a miniature car and a small purse into the compartment and talked about how we sometimes buy things in our attempts to find contentment. She tried a dollar bill; it fit into the compartment when folded but didn't make the doll work.

We may think with enough money, we'll finally be happy, but we know in our hearts it's not true.

None of those things were ever meant to fulfill us. God made us, and He alone knows what will bring us contentment. True contentment can only come through a relationship with God and by living to glorify Him.

ༀ 7 ༁

Godly Priorities

A rmed with a proper, spiritual perspective about our possessions and our lives, we can now turn our attention to our priorities. The Bible gives us the inspiration and the tools we need to make sure our lives line up with a proper spiritual perspective. As Christians, our priorities should be the same as God's priorities. We need to make sure our walk (our actions) matches our talk (what we say we believe). After all, the true measure of a person's priorities is not what they say, but what they do. Our actions are the best indicators of what we value. James 1:22 reminds us to not merely listen to the word, but to do what it says. Consider your actions as you read these challenging passages from God's Word.

Bigger Barns

We'll begin with one of Jesus' most powerful parables. Traditionally called "The Parable of the Rich Fool," this passage from Luke 12 is so appropriate to our current culture and our abundance of possessions. God's word is truly timeless. Even though this was written to a culture where rich people were relatively rare, it is even more relevant today to a culture where wealth is commonplace. Isn't the timelessness of God's Word impressive? These words were written thousands of years ago but still apply to us in the 21st century.

Let's set the stage for this passage. Jesus is in a familiar position, surrounded by crowds eager to see what's going on, hoping to watch a miraculous healing or to just see this famous and controversial man in action. Just before the passage begins, Jesus is teaching His disciples when a man in the crowd interrupts Him to ask a question. Apparently, the man was involved in a family dispute. He wanted Jesus to get involved as well by telling his brother to divide the father's estate with him. Consistent with Jesus' habits, He took the opportunity to not just address the particular situation, but to teach an underlying principle with a story.

> Teacher, tell my brother to divide the inheritance with me." Jesus replied, "Man, who appointed me a judge or an arbiter between you?" Then he said to them, "Watch out! Be on your guard against all kinds of greed; life does not consist in an abundance of possessions. And he told them this parable:
>
> The ground of a certain rich man yielded an abundant harvest. He thought to himself, 'What shall I do? I have no place to store my crops.'
>
> Then he said, 'This is what I'll do. I will tear down my barns and build bigger ones, and there I will store my surplus grain. And I'll say to myself, "You have plenty of grain laid up for many years. Take life easy; eat, drink and be merry." '

But God said to him, 'You fool! This very night your life will be demanded from you. Then who will get what you have prepared for yourself?'

This is how it will be with whoever stores up things for themselves but is not rich toward God.

Luke 12:13–21 (NIV)

Jesus' statement "life does not consist in an abundance of possessions" is just as true today as it was when He walked the earth. But while the concepts are timeless, the specifics of the parable may not be relatable. I doubt you know many (or any) farmers struggling to decide what to do with their excess crops from an abundant harvest. But we all most certainly know many people who have an abundance of possessions. That group of people with an excess of possessions most likely includes ourselves. Perhaps these changes suggested by my husband Eric will bring a more modern feel to the passage:

A certain rich man had a 401K that yielded an abundant return. He thought to himself, 'What shall I do? I have no place to store all my stuff.'

Then he said, 'This is what I'll do. I'll rent a storage unit, and then I'll have room to store my surplus stuff. And I'll say to myself, "You have plenty of stuff laid up for many years. Take life easy; eat, drink and be merry!"'

But God said to him, 'You fool! This very night your life will be demanded from you. Then who will get what you have prepared for yourself?'

This is how it will be with whoever stores up things for themselves but is not rich toward God.

Luke 12:16–21
(Eric Hyche's updates to the NIV)

From an earthly perspective, this man appears to have it made. He'll be able to slack off on his work now, confident he's got plenty stored up for the next few seasons. He might be able to finally spend time relaxing, or maybe pick up a new hobby. His family, friends, and neighbors are probably a little jealous; they'd love to be able to take it easy, too. They might be considering asking for a gift or a loan.

When we look at the situation from a Christian perspective, however, there are obvious problems. Whether it's grain stored in barns or surplus stuff stored in storage units, the issues are the same, and Jesus confronts them boldly. There are several problems with this man's attitude and his solution to his storage problem. He viewed his crops, his barn, and his farm as his possessions, earned by his work, and used for his own present and future needs. He gives no thanks or glory to God for the abundant harvest. He doesn't mention the option of sharing anything. His ultimate goal appears to be a life of comfort and ease. He is greedy, selfish, and lazy, and his priorities are completely focused on himself. He is putting his faith in his possessions with no acknowledgement of God.

It's easy to disregard this passage by assuming it only applies to those with an abundance. This is a short-sighted view. The volume of the man's possessions isn't necessarily the problem. The parable would work even if the amount of possessions occupied much less space than a barn. The real issues are related to the reasons he stored up his possessions and how he planned to use them. Ultimately, the crux of this man's problem is that God doesn't even factor into the equation of his life.

Consider again God's reaction to this man's situation:

> But God said to him, 'You fool! You will die this very night. Then who will get everything you worked for?'
>
> Yes, a person is a fool to store up earthly wealth but not have a rich relationship with God.
>
> Luke 12:20–21 (NIV)

The rich fool had it all planned out; a life of ease and financial security awaited him. He never considered it could all be taken away in the blink of an eye. His wealth was useless because his security was based on something that could never last. The parable is a sobering reminder that our relationship with God is the only thing that really matters and the only thing on which we can depend.

What about you? What are you storing up? How do you view your skills, your opportunities, and your possessions? Do you prioritize your relationship with God? If someone studied the details of your life, including how you spend your money and your time, what conclusion would they make about what's important to you? Don't be a fool. Put your trust, your time, and your heart into the only thing that really matters. If we could strip away everything inconsequential, everything

> **Our relationship with God is the only thing that really matters and the only thing on which we can depend.**

that is optional and unnecessary, we might finally understand that our ultimate goal is to love God and to love others.

Sell Treasure, Gain Treasure

Jesus had plenty to say about our attitude towards our possessions. In Matthew 19, Jesus encounters a man who wants a guarantee of eternal life, but he thinks the way to earn it is by doing good deeds. He asks Jesus what good deed he needs to do to earn eternal life. Jesus answers by telling him to keep the commandments, so the man asks which ones, just to be sure. Jesus lists a few (murder, adultery, stealing, lying, honoring parents, loving your neighbor). So far so good, because apparently, he had a long track record of obedience to all of these commandments. He must have been feeling pretty confident at this point. Wanting to be absolutely sure, he asks if there is anything else he needs to do. Knowing the man's heart, Jesus cut directly to the one issue holding him back from full obedience.

> Jesus answered, 'If you want to be perfect, go, sell your possessions and give to the poor, and you will have treasure in heaven. Then come, follow me.' When the young man heard this, he went away sad, because he had great wealth. Then Jesus said to his disciples, 'Truly I tell you, it is hard for someone who is rich to enter the kingdom of heaven. Again I tell you, it is easier for a camel to go through the eye of a needle than for someone who is rich to enter the kingdom of God.'
>
> Matthew 19:21–24 (NIV)

You have to admire the boldness of this man as he approaches Jesus to ask what he needed to do. He had lived a good life, but he wanted to make sure he was doing everything he needed to do and had all of the proper boxes checked. He must have breathed a small sigh of relief when Jesus rattled off the list of commandments, knowing he had already checked those off. I don't know about you, but I wouldn't have felt so secure after hearing the list; I can't honestly say I've obeyed all of those commandments. I've told some lies. I haven't always honored my parents or loved my neighbor as myself.

Jesus always knows how to cut to the chase, to get to the real issue. In this man's case, the real issue was his possessions. Jesus knew this was the one thing holding him back. He told him, "If you want to be perfect, go and sell all your possessions and give the money to the poor, and you will have treasure in heaven. Then come, follow me." Notice the paradox: by giving away his treasures (his possessions) and giving the money to the poor, he would be gaining treasure (in heaven). Again, Jesus reminds us that only what we've "invested" in our spiritual lives will last.

Does this mean we need to sell everything we have and donate the money to the poor? Probably not. It's not likely we'll be called on to make such an extreme choice. But if God asked us to, could we? It depends on how we view our possessions. Similarly to the rich fool, if we believe our possessions belong to us and that we earned them, we're more likely to hang onto them tightly. However, if we acknowledge they belong to God and they're only "ours" temporarily, and if we're committed to using them in whatever way God calls us to use them, we won't hold on so tightly.

The story from Matthew 19 is a clear example of how our possessions can get in the way of our relationship with God. If we really want to focus on serving God, our possessions can be a hindrance. In Hebrews 12, we are urged to get rid of anything that holds us back from serving Him wholeheartedly.

Throwing Off Obstacles

> Therefore, since we are surrounded by such a great cloud of witnesses, let us throw off everything that hinders and the sin that so easily entangles. And let us run with perseverance the race marked out for us, fixing our eyes on Jesus, the pioneer and perfecter of faith. For the joy set before him he endured the cross, scorning its shame, and sat down at the right hand of the throne of God. Consider him who endured such opposition from sinners, so that you will not grow weary and lose heart.
>
> Hebrews 12:1–2 (NIV)

This passage in Hebrews 12 follows right after the famous Faith Chapter of Hebrews 11, a long list of the exploits of some of God's most impressive followers. This is the "great cloud of witnesses" that surrounds us, cheering us on and encouraging us that we too can live out our faith. We are encouraged to "throw off everything that hinders and the sin that so easily entangles" as we focus on Jesus and run the race marked out for us. Let's explore what this verse might mean practically.

It's not hard to see how sin could trip us up on the race. Sin is literally a walk in the opposite direction of where God leads us. Nothing could get us more entangled and off-course than sin. We could be led astray by anything from gossip to stealing to idolatry. God knows our weaknesses. Satan especially knows what will most easily tempt us to go against God's commandments. It's not difficult to understand this part of the passage, although it's not always easy to avoid the entanglement of sin.

What about "let us throw off everything that hinders?" What does that mean? This passage reminds me of a Bible study we hosted in the late 1980s in our Atlanta apartment. Eric was leading the study and came up with a great illustration for this verse. He volunteered two of the Bible study group members to compete in a race around our apartment building. Both of them were young, fit, and competitive, and they were both determined to win. Eric outlined the rules and their path, but before sending them on their way, he told one of the racers, our friend Jennifer, that she had to carry something with her. I don't remember exactly what he gave Jennifer to carry (and neither does Eric), but she figured out the best way to hold the item and still win the race. Just before starting the race, he stopped them again and added another item for her to carry. This process continued until she was barely able to hold everything. At this point, there was really no point in them actually completing the race as she had no chance of winning.

This is an extreme example, but it illustrates the point well. And since we're talking about clutter, it is especially useful. Jennifer didn't need any of the items Eric made her hold. She needed to be as unencumbered as possible so she could run quickly. Those items would slow her down. Her best chance of victory was to literally act out the verse, to "throw off everything that hinders."

> Clutter is a
> burden we
> were never
> meant to bear.

Our clutter is hindering us, keeping us from living the life God intends for us. We can't effectively focus on glorifying God and serving others when we are distracted by our clutter. In Chapter 3, I shared many specific examples of my clutter and its consequences. My schedule clutter and attention clutter were huge hindrances to my attempts to live for God. These same distractions occur with physical clutter. We spend hours sorting through piles of stuff when our time could be used to serve others. We spend money on unnecessary purchases when our money could be used to further God's kingdom.

We're trying to navigate our lives carrying a whole lot of unnecessary stuff. Our clutter, whether it's physical, schedule, or attention clutter, is weighing us down. It's holding us back from the life God has planned for us. Clutter is a burden we have placed on ourselves that we were never meant to bear. It's time to get serious about throwing it off.

Where's Your Treasure?

How do we know what we value? This is an important question to answer. What we value or treasure is a gauge of our priorities.

> Do not store up for yourselves treasures on earth, where moths and vermin destroy, and where thieves break in and steal. But store up for yourselves treasures in heaven, where moths and vermin do not destroy, and where thieves do not

break in and steal. For where your treasure is, there your heart will be also.

No one can serve two masters. Either you will hate the one and love the other, or you will be devoted to the one and despise the other. You cannot serve both God and money.

Matthew 6:19–21, 24 (NIV)

When I read the phrase "store up," my mind automatically goes to piles of clutter in homes and rented storage units. "Storing up treasures on earth" undoubtedly applies to our habits of accumulating physical clutter. Again in this passage, Jesus exhorts us to prioritize treasures in heaven over treasures on earth. He reminds us that treasures in heaven are everlasting, while treasures on earth can be stolen or destroyed by vermin (insects or animals like rodents). What we treasure reveals the true state of our hearts.

Jesus' statement "you cannot serve both God and money" has always scared me a little bit. It's so absolute and stated so strongly. We would do well to pay attention to such an admonition. Consider the words of John Piper, well-known Christian author and preacher, "Jesus spoke more about money than he did about sex, heaven, and hell. Money is a big deal to Jesus. There must be something really dangerous about money."[15] I don't know about you, but I find it both surprising and disturbing that Jesus talked about money more than He did about heaven and hell. When it comes to our relationship with money, we'd better get this right.

> What we treasure reveals the true state of our hearts.

Continuing in the same article by John Piper, this is how he explains the concepts of serving money and serving God: "To serve money means to calculate all of your behaviors, all of your life, to maximize what money can give you, always asking what benefits can come to you from money. That would be serving money...serving God would mean doing everything you do, calculating all your behavior to maximize the pleasures you can get from God, all the benefits you can get from God in Christ."

I won't debate about what this means practically because I can't judge anyone's life but my own. Only God knows all of our actions and the motivations for them. On the one hand, I don't believe we should all just throw caution to the wind, not making any plans for our children's future or our retirement and donating every penny to charity instead. On the other hand, how can we feel protected from admonishment if we have spent money with abandon and have collected piles of clutter to show for it? The key takeaway is that each of us needs to examine our hearts to figure out where our treasure lies.

What Makes You Rich?

Continuing the discussion on what we treasure, consider these verses in I Timothy 6 written by Paul to his assistant, Timothy, who is leading the church in Ephesus in Paul's absence. Paul is giving Timothy instruction on what to teach as he leads the church. When Paul speaks about "laying up treasure," he isn't just referring to money or possessions. Again, the crux of the matter is our priorities.

"Command those who are rich in this present world not to be arrogant nor to put their hope in wealth, which is so uncertain, but to put their hope in God, who richly provides us with everything for our enjoyment. Command them to do good, to be rich in good deeds, and to be generous and willing to share. In this way they will lay up treasure for themselves as a firm foundation for the coming age, so that they may take hold of the life that is truly life."

I Timothy 6:17–19 (NIV)

Paul reminds Timothy that our possessions are temporary and uncertain, and they don't produce contentment. Not only that, but the love of money can lead us to actions that can separate us from God. Paul encourages Timothy to flee from this love of money, to pursue godly character, and to remember God's promise of eternal life in Him. Timothy is called to teach the people to put their hope in God, not in earthly riches. He advises them to share their time and their possessions ("to do good, to be rich in good deeds, and to be generous and willing to share"). I love how Timothy is to remind the rich to be rich in good deeds! This is yet another reminder to store our treasure in heaven, not on earth.

Don't Love the World

As Christians, we know there's so much more to our lives than what we see right in front of us. We're part of the world, but we also know deep in our hearts that this earthly life is temporary.

Do not love the world or anything in the world. If anyone loves the world, love for the Father is not in them. For everything in the world—the lust of

> the flesh, the lust of the eyes, and the pride of life—comes not from the Father but from the world. The world and its desires pass away, but whoever does the will of God lives forever.
>
> I John 2:15–17 (NIV)

I have read this passage in the NIV many times and wondered about the phrase "the pride of life." I tried another translation hoping for clarity. Consider the same passage from the New Living Translation:

> Do not love this world nor the things it offers you, for when you love the world, you do not have the love of the Father in you. For the world offers only a craving for physical pleasure, a craving for everything we see, and pride in our achievements and possessions. These are not from the Father, but are from this world. And this world is fading away, along with everything that people crave. But anyone who does what pleases God will live forever.
>
> I John 2:15–17 (NLT)

Just when I thought this passage wasn't too difficult to obey, I found this translation with "pride in our achievements and possessions" in place of "the pride of life." And just like that, I am led to a deeper level of understanding and a realization that I am not living up to my beliefs.

You see, taking pride in my possessions isn't a big issue for me, but taking pride in my achievements is another story. Taking pride in my achievements is not from God. Taking pride in my achievements is a symptom of loving the world.

I am ashamed to admit that I revel in my accomplishments. As a driven and competitive person, I like being recognized for attaining my goals. This longing is manifested in a desire to be the best at whatever I set out to do, be it academics, athletics, or just about anything. I can turn anything into a competition and often do. And I am a terrible loser.

As far as our discussion of clutter, this need for acknowledgement can be lumped into the category of attention clutter. This "look at me" attitude goes squarely against God's word. I need constant reminders that the only person whose opinion of me really matters is God's. The only talent I have comes from God. The only achievement that really matters and will last beyond this world is what I do for God. It doesn't mean I can't continue to do my best at whatever I do. It does mean my motivation needs to be glorifying God and serving Him as I serve those around me. Others need to reap the benefits, and God needs to get the credit and the attention, not me.

Our Soul is Priceless

A worldly perspective and a godly perspective are often light years away from each other. Even the disciples struggled with the discrepancy.

> Then Jesus said to his disciples, 'Whoever wants to be my disciple must deny themselves and take up their cross and follow me. For whoever wants to save their life will lose it, but whoever loses their life for me will find it. What good will it be for someone to gain the whole world, yet forfeit their soul? Or what can anyone give in exchange for their soul?'
>
> Matthew 16:24–26 (NLT)

Imagine being told by Jesus you had to take up your cross to follow Him. Crucifixion was a common form of punishment at the time. Taking up your cross was essentially heading straight to your death. And lest they turn and run to save their own lives, Jesus informed them that only by giving up their lives for Him would their lives be saved. What a contradiction!

In the last verse, Jesus compares the worth of the entire world to the worth of one soul. Matthew Henry's explanation in his commentary[16] is so helpful for understanding this passage. In spiritual terms, one soul is worth more than all of the world. Our own soul is of greater value than all of the money, possessions, power, fame, and pleasures of this world. If anyone has the right to make this judgement, it is Jesus. God created the world and everything in it, so He knows the world's value. Jesus alone knows the value of our souls because He knows the price He had to pay on the cross to save our souls.

What if you could have literally everything you've ever wanted—your dream job, the relationships you've always wanted, talents and skills far beyond your current abilities, a home custom-designed for your needs with exquisite decor, the most advanced self-driving automobile, a new wardrobe from your favorite clothier, a best-selling book, a starring role in a hit movie, etc. Oh, and the price tag for this reads "$0.00," and you get it all through free delivery tomorrow, even if you're not an Amazon Prime member.

Does it sound too good to be true? Even if this were possible, this unimaginable gift might come with a huge price tag. It might not cost you any money, but it could very well cost your soul. It could be that along with all of these incredible free gifts, you and your spouse are now working 60+ hours a week keeping up with your job and everything else. You don't have time for church, volunteer work to serve others, or reflection on your life. If you were handed every single item on a list of your hopes and dreams and you could live a carefree life from here on out, how likely is it that you would keep your focus on the eternal? If your life were perfect, it would be much easier to love the world. Loving God and glorifying Him with your life wouldn't be impossible, but it would definitely be much more difficult.

Though you and I would be sorely tempted to take this offer without looking back, Jesus unequivocally warns us that it's absolutely not worth it. "Is anything worth more than your soul?" asks Jesus. Clearly the answer is, "No."

I grew up in a Christian home. I heard Bible stories in church throughout my life. I knew from a young age that Jesus died on the cross to save us from our sins so we could spend eternity with God in heaven. But I'll never forget the day I finally understood the gravity of that truth. Not long after we were married, Eric and I were attending a church Bible study in which the leader was equipping us to study the Bible with people who hadn't yet been taught about Jesus. One evening, we were discussing a Bible study about Jesus' death on the cross. After explaining the details of Jesus' crucifixion, the study leader said something like this, "Even if you were the only person in the world, Jesus would still have had to die. He would have done it just for you." And then came the follow up question: "If you were the only one, who would have nailed him there?"

It's one thing to say, "Jesus died for the sins of the world," but it's fundamentally different to say he died for *my* sins. I began to study more about the crucifixion and about sin in the weeks to come. I had grown up in a Christian home and had been taught right and wrong. I had always obeyed the rules, walked the straight and narrow. But I had never come face to face with my inward sin, the "sins of the heart": pride, jealousy, selfish ambition, fits of rage, envy, etc. Those sins, my sins, had been responsible for putting Jesus on the cross. Jesus considered my soul worth the price.

Going back to our earlier question and Scripture, what if I really could "gain the whole world" (get anything I want in the world), but I would have to lose my soul in the process? Without a doubt, it wouldn't be worth it. It would trivialize and dishonor what Jesus did for me, like spitting in the face of Jesus' sacrifice.

Here's the clincher. You and I won't ever have to make the decision of whether to trade our soul for this "gift" of anything we want. But every day, with our small decisions, we make choices that define the direction of our lives. We decide whether to value the things of this world or the things of God. We store up treasure every day, either treasure on earth or treasure in heaven. We make choices that either prioritize our relationships on earth or our relationship with God. We choose whether to keep our time, money, and possessions for ourselves or whether to share them with others. We choose whether to get rid of the clutter holding us back from our walk with Christ. We choose to put God first and trust Him to meet our needs (or not). We're either serving God or serving money. Our daily actions can resemble trying to stuff the playhouse people, the car, or a dollar bill into the God-shaped hole in our lives.

If someone didn't know you and watched the way you spend your time and money, what would they conclude about your priorities? Do you make choices that value your soul and the price Jesus paid for it?

In his book *Sharing Possessions: What Faith Demands,* Luke Timothy Johnson shares some practical questions to assist us in our self-reflection. I found these questions very powerful and use them frequently. Questions such as these can help us identify what we value. How would you honestly answer these questions?

- What drives me? When I wake up in the morning, what is it that motivates me to get going? What am I excited to wake up and do?

- What will I always make time to do, even if I have a busy schedule?

- On what do I base my success? When I look at my peers and compare myself, do I base that comparison on my looks, my job, my position, my family, my level of recognition, my finances, my health?

- How do I decide whether I've had a successful day (or week or year)? What makes me feel good about what I've accomplished?[17]

I encourage you to seriously consider these questions. Be honest with yourself and with God about your answers. You might be able to fool someone else, but God knows your heart. As painful as it might be to acknowledge where you stand, only when you are willing to face the truth can you make real changes. Spend time in prayer, asking God to reveal anything you need to address.

We've looked at Scripture about our possessions and talked in great detail about how we view our possessions. We know examining our heart and our attitude is paramount in evaluating our priorities. But we also have to consider how we're using our possessions on a practical basis. Recognizing everything we have is ultimately from God, what does God want us to do with the belongings He has entrusted to us during our time on earth?

Good Stewards

In biblical terms, we are *stewards*. Steward isn't a word we use frequently, but the concept is a familiar one. In biblical times, a steward acted similarly to what we think of as a manager today. Stewards were given responsibility for managing a home and its affairs, including finances, servants, crops, etc. Stewards understood they didn't own anything they were managing. They didn't have the freedom to make unilateral or selfish decisions about how to manage the household. Their responsibility was to manage the household in the way their masters desired.

Here is a story from my own life that is applicable to the concept of stewardship. Several years ago, Eric and I planned to mulch our yard one Saturday. We didn't own a truck at the time, so we borrowed our neighbor's truck. It took the better part of the day to load, unload, and spread the mulch. We filled the truck's gas tank and returned it that evening.

The next day, our neighbor told us his truck had a new scratch on the side. Since we had only taken the truck to the mulch place and back and had stayed with the truck the entire time, we were shocked. We had no idea how it could have happened. But our neighbor took good care of his vehicles, and he wasn't the kind of person who would make up a story. The truck had been damaged while in our care, and although we couldn't explain how it had happened, we knew paying for the damage was the right thing to do. We learned a valuable lesson that day about being extremely careful with possessions loaned to us.

God has graciously given us so much to enjoy. Since we are stewards, not owners, we have a responsibility to treat everything God has given us with respect. We need to use what we've been given according to God's desires and purposes.

When we returned the truck to our neighbor with a scratch on it, we had to take responsibility for the damage that happened while it was under our care. In a similar vein, one day all of us will be judged for how well we took care of the gifts God gave us. We will have to give an account of how we managed not only our physical belongings, but our time, money, talents, relationships, and positions.

The Parable of the Talents from Matthew 25 illustrates stewardship well. Jesus told the story of a master who was going on a trip and entrusted three servants with his money while he was gone. He gave each servant a different amount based on the servant's abilities. When the master returned, he confronted each servant to find out how they had handled the money while he was gone. The servant who got five bags of silver had invested the money and earned five more bags. The master was thrilled with his efforts and gave him even more responsibility. The servant who got two bags of silver had also invested the money and doubled the amount. The master also praised him and gave him more responsibility. But the servant who got only one bag of silver didn't do so well. He was afraid he would lose the money, so he hid it. When he returned the money after the master got back, the master was furious!

> His master replied, 'You wicked, lazy servant! So you knew that I harvest where I have not sown and gather where I have not scattered seed? Well then, you should have put my money on deposit with the bankers, so that when I returned I would have received it back with interest.'
>
> Matthew 25:26–27 (NLT)

All three of these servants were stewards of some of the master's money. They were all entrusted with a different amount, according to their abilities. The master didn't expect the same results from each of them in terms of monetary return. However, he did expect each of them to put the money to good use. He expected to receive some return on investment from each one.

I used to think the third servant who hid the money so he wouldn't lose it was punished too severely. After all, I can totally relate to him. I am notorious for losing things (not a very steward-like quality, I know). He returned the money in the same condition he had received it, so why were his actions judged so harshly? It's because a good steward is supposed to manage what's entrusted to him in the way his master chooses, not the way the steward thinks is best. A good steward knows his master well enough to know what is expected. And a good steward works hard and doesn't take the easy way out. Clearly, the third servant wasn't a good steward.

What does this concept mean in terms of our physical possessions? We would all agree that if we are good stewards of our possessions, we would be careful not to lose them, damage them, waste them, or destroy them. We would be willing to share them, recognizing they were given to us by God. It also means we should put them to good use in a way that glorifies God.

How do good stewards use their time? They don't spend all of their time on activities that only benefit themselves. Good stewards of time devote significant portions of their time to serving others. They are aware of the needs around them and are willing to take the time to meet those needs. They are intentional in using their time to glorify God.

Sharing Possessions, Talents, & Time

Most of us are blessed to have far more than we need to just survive. Whether we're talking about possessions, talents, or time, God's intention is that we should be willing to share. Sometimes sharing comes naturally, especially if we're sharing with someone we love.

But what about sharing with people we don't know? What about sharing with someone who is considered your enemy? One of the most well-known passages in the Bible, the Parable of the Good Samaritan in Luke 10, presents this exact scenario. Before we dive into this story, let's consider the context.

We notice right off the bat that Jesus told this parable to answer the question of a religious leader, an expert in the law. He asked Jesus what he needed to do to get to heaven. It's likely that his motive was to trap Jesus into contradicting the law (a common practice for the religious experts) or to show off his knowledge of the law (another common practice). You see, the religious leader was already sure of his salvation. He wanted justification for the way he had been living. And just like always, Jesus knew exactly what the man was thinking, so Jesus turned the question right back to him.

> He answered, 'Love the Lord your God with all your heart and with all your soul and with all your strength and with all your mind'; and, 'Love your neighbor as yourself.'
>
> 'You have answered correctly,' Jesus replied. 'Do this and you will live.'
>
> But he wanted to justify himself, so he asked Jesus, 'And who is my neighbor?'
>
> Luke 10:27–29 (NIV)

The man asked for some clarification of the word neighbor. Since we are given the hint "the man wanted to justify his actions," we can assume he hadn't been very inclusive in his love for his neighbors. He was likely hoping Jesus would define neighbor narrowly, excluding the types of people the man had already been excluding. Just as He does many times in Scripture, Jesus answered with a story.

A Jew was traveling from Jerusalem to Jericho. On the way, he was attacked, robbed, and left for dead beside the road. Three men encounter the Jew beside the road. First a priest saw him and crossed over to the other side of the road and kept going. Then a temple assistant did the same thing. Finally, a Samaritan came along, saw the man, and had compassion on him. He did his best to treat his wounds, then took him to a nearby inn and left him in the care of an innkeeper, paying him to take care of the Jew.

No matter how many times you've read this story, don't miss the powerful teaching of Jesus. Isn't it ironic that neither of the two religious people in the story, the priest and the temple assistant, do anything to help the man? They walk right by him, even crossing to the other side of the road to get as far away from him as possible.

The priest and temple assistant were fellow Jews. If one of the three people in this story were going to help, you'd expect it to be one of them. Samaritans and Jews were bitter enemies. The hatred between these two groups was so intense that sometimes Jews would travel two extra days just to avoid going near Samaritans. But the Samaritan not only offers him help, but goes the extra mile to pay for an innkeeper to house and care for the man after he leaves.

Unselfish giving irrespective of differences is the standard God uses to judge our own giving. God wants us to share our gifts with anyone in need, no matter how unlike us that person may be. Quite a challenge indeed.

The Good Samaritan provides a worthy model of service, but just as always, Jesus is the ultimate model. He didn't just give what he had; he gave himself completely. Jesus literally laid down His life for us, and he calls us to do the same for others. He wants us to "walk the walk" by loving with actions and not just with our words.

> This is how we know what love is: Jesus Christ laid down his life for us. And we ought to lay down our lives for our brothers and sisters. If anyone has

material possessions and sees a brother or sister in need but has no pity on them, how can the love of God be in that person? Dear children, let us not love with words or speech but with actions and in truth.

I John 3:16–18 (NIV)

One day we will have to give an account for how we utilized God's gifts. God will judge our level of stewardship against the standard of His Word. When we encounter a needy person, perhaps we should picture this person as Jesus instead so we won't hesitate. God defines our giving to others just as if we were giving directly to Him.

Each of us is in a unique situation, and we can't judge each other's hearts and motives. The only one who knows our heart is God. My prayer is that we could comprehend the depth of God's love for us and the lavishness of the gifts He's given us, that each of us would examine ourselves in light of God's Word, and that we would unselfishly share our possessions, our talents, and our time with anyone in need. Consider the unselfishness of the Good Samaritan, who was willing to come to the rescue of someone far outside his social circle. Above all, consider Jesus, who literally gave up his life for both those who would follow Him and those who had nailed Him to the cross. We are never more Christlike than when we give.

> We are never more Christlike than when we give.

৪ 8 ষ

God's Promises

When faced with a difficult task, we are often tempted to ask, "Why should I do this? How do I know it will work? What's in it for me?" Let's face it—no one wants to endure the painful process of change without some kind of guarantee it will be worth it. If we deal with our physical clutter by donating what we aren't using, how do we know that we won't be in need later? If we use our God-given abilities and our time to benefit others, will there be enough time to take care of our families? Will we still have time for fun and relaxing activities? God knows us so well. He knows we need reassurance. He has given us plenty of promises to fuel our efforts.

Put God First and He'll Take Care of Us

During the Sermon on the Mount, Jesus issued some serious challenges to His followers, including a command to store up treasures in heaven, not on earth. Jesus already understands our temptation to stock up so we won't have to worry about running out of food, drink, or clothes. He promises if we put Him first, He'll take care of us, just as God takes care of the birds and the flowers. The passage speaks directly to two very commonly voiced objections to decluttering: "But I might need this someday" and "I had better keep it, just in case."

> So do not worry, saying, 'What shall we eat?' or 'What shall we drink?' or 'What shall we wear?' For the pagans run after all these things, and your heavenly Father knows that you need them. But seek first his kingdom and his righteousness, and all these things will be given to you as well.
>
> Matthew 6:31–33 (NIV)

For those of you who use the NIV predominantly, I'd like to include another version of this passage. Sometimes when we've heard a scripture multiple times, we don't really "hear it" anymore until it's worded differently.

> So don't worry about these things, saying, 'What will we eat? What will we drink? What will we wear?' These things dominate the thoughts of unbelievers, but your heavenly Father already knows all your needs. Seek the Kingdom of God above all else, and live righteously, and he will give you everything you need.
>
> Matthew 6:31–33 (NLT)

Wow! Do you really believe if you seek God and His Kingdom first, He will make sure you have everything you need? If we really believed it, how would it change the way we live? I don't think I've personally ever seriously put God to the test on this promise. How about you?

When I think about people who have put this promise to the test and have seen God make good on it, the first people that come to mind are my friends Donna and Phil Waldron. Eric and I met Phil and Donna while we were living in Atlanta. Soon after meeting them, they moved to Cozumel, Mexico to start a home for orphaned and abandoned children. Ciudad de Angeles (City of Angels) began with nine children in three rental homes in 2002 and has since grown into a multi-home campus with 30-40 children.[18] In 2008, the Waldrons followed God's call to be missionaries in Western Honduras. They are the leaders of Mission Upreach, a dynamic ministry committed to serving the poor and underserved and to helping establish new, self-sustaining churches.[19] We have been fortunate to support Ciudad de Angeles as sponsors of one of the children (now a young adult) and to now support Mission Upreach. Time and time again, we have seen Phil and Donna launch a new ministry, often at their own personal expense and risk, trusting God would take care of their needs. I asked Donna to share her story as an example of living out this passage.

My daily struggle is fully believing the promise contained in this text. One would think after years of experiencing this truth over and over again, I would be better at it; but instead, I feel like a beginner each time I face a new challenge. I believe God wants me to let go of my striving and doing and simply trust Him fully. He is either able and faithful, or He is not. There's no half-time God, nor is God with us one day and not the next. His love is solid and real and present and active. He really is all we need.

More than a few times in our life on the mission field, we have faced impossible odds. Almost always it was related to funding. Because our mission funding comes from churches and individuals who give generously towards our efforts, it is easy to forget we are not dependent on people, but on God using people to accomplish his work. We're not all called to leave father, mother, brother, sister, and the comforts of our homeland to go do missions. I think some are called to sacrificially give of their lives and some of their money and some of their prayers and encouragement. I am personally grateful to God that our family was called to go. I love serving on the mission field. For me, the mission life strips me of many distractions and keeps me focused on my God-given purpose. Sometimes when I step back into the US for a brief visit, I am overwhelmed with the challenges of the social pressures of money and possessions and the busyness that so many families face. After a glimpse of that life, I gladly return to my life of simplicity and focus. I feel so blessed that my calling involves stepping away from the things that can consume life and leave one feeling empty and purposeless.

A struggle many have (including myself) is misunderstanding what being blessed and provided for by God looks like. We want it to meet our expectations and desires. We want it to consist only of good things. He promises the provision of what we need, which is often far less than what we want. Learning to fully trust him involves learning to see life and people and challenges as He does.

In 2015, our son was involved in an accident that resulted in a traumatic brain injury, leaving him 100% dependent on his young wife. God's provision did not look like healing, but rather provision to survive the family trauma, one day at a time. And as usual, God has and will continue to redeem our circumstances and pain for His purposes so that we are privileged to participate in bringing His Kingdom to earth. We serve a God of redemption and provision. Trust Him and allow him to show you just how good He is. Fully trusting God is believing, in spite of my circumstances, that God is in control and I can believe Him at his word. (D. Waldron, personal communication, October 22, 2019)

The Promise of an Abundant Life

When you think of the word "abundance," what comes to mind? For many, "abundance" translates to wealth or plentiful possessions. But God never promised His followers would be wealthy or loaded with possessions.

In John 10, Jesus likens Himself to a Good Shepherd who knows the sheep, calls them by name, and protects them by laying down His life for them. He contrasts the good shepherd to a thief, who comes only to steal, kill, and destroy. He follows with these words:

> The thief comes only to steal and kill and destroy; I have come that they may have life, and have it to the full.
>
> John 10:10 (NIV)

The full life God promises doesn't refer to wealth. We've all heard stories of televangelists who promise great wealth to those who support their campaigns and dupe unaware viewers into emptying their bank accounts to contribute. But that's not what Jesus means in this passage, and it's certainly not what God promises anywhere in the Scripture. Although there are certainly Biblical examples of wealthy followers of God like Solomon, there are at least as many examples of those who weren't wealthy from an earthly standpoint.

An abundant life from God gives us contentment, peace, and joy, even when our life circumstances may look anything but peaceful. Paul endured more than we could imagine, yet he was content. An abundant life with God gives us an eternal perspective on every life situation.

> Do not be anxious about anything, but in every situation, by prayer and petition, with thanksgiving, present your requests to God. And the peace of God, which transcends all understanding, will guard your hearts and your minds in Christ Jesus.
>
> I have learned the secret of being content in any and every situation, whether well fed or hungry, whether living in plenty or in want. I can do all this through him who gives me strength.
>
> Philippians 4:6–7, 12–13 (NIV)

God promises to take care of us, to always have our best interests at heart, and to always be with us, no matter what the circumstances. Throughout the Bible, we are reminded that God will never leave us or forsake us. What a comfort!

> So do not fear, for I am with you; do not be
> dismayed, for I am your God. I will strengthen you
> and help you; I will uphold you with my righteous
> right hand.
>
> Isaiah 41:10 (NIV)

The abundant life God promises includes eternal life with Him in heaven. No matter what we must endure on earth, we can rest assured in our ultimate reward, spending eternity with our Heavenly Father. This is truly the most wonderful gift we could ever receive.

> For the wages of sin is death, but the gift of
> God is eternal life in Christ Jesus our Lord.
>
> Romans 6:23 (NIV)

The Promise of Using Every Situation for Good

Additionally, God doesn't promise we won't go through difficult times. Even when we put God first and follow His lead, we aren't guaranteed a life of ease. Remember Paul's description of contentment we just read? Keep in mind that Paul endured extreme hunger and thirst, was exposed to extreme weather conditions, was shipwrecked three times, tortured multiple times (with whips, rods, and stones), betrayed, and imprisoned. And Paul was one of God's most devoted followers! God helped Paul through all of these situations, no matter how dire. He used Paul to bring thousands of people to God, and He is still using Paul's story and Paul's words to inspire us today.

Just like Paul, we will likely have to endure hardships. Christians are by no means immune to trouble. Bad things do happen to good people. Many times, we won't understand why we're going through dark times. In fact, in some situations, we may never understand until we get to heaven. But we can rest assured that God will use every single circumstance in our lives for good. As followers of God, we can be assured that when we put Him first, He will work all things for good. Revel in God's promises to us from Romans 8:

> And we know that in all things God works for the good of those who love him, who have been called according to his purpose.
>
> No, in all these things we are more than conquerors through him who loved us. For I am convinced that neither death nor life, neither angels nor demons, neither the present nor the future, nor any powers, neither height nor depth, nor anything else in all creation, will be able to separate us from the love of God that is in Christ Jesus our Lord.
>
> Romans 8:28, 37–39 (NIV)

What beautiful reassurance. Doesn't this passage just make you want to stand up and yell "Amen!"?

Remember that no matter where we are in our journey with God, He is always waiting for us, longing to be closer and to show us abundant life. God wants only the best for us. He longs for us to know Him and to trust Him. He has great plans for our lives. He knows what we've unsuccessfully used to try to fill that God-shaped hole. And He is waiting for us to discover an abundant life with Him.

༄ 9 ༅

What Does a Godly Relationship Look Like?

So far in our discussion, we've painted a picture of an unhealthy relationship with our possessions. We've examined the negative effects of clutter. We've studied Biblical precepts that can guide us in making more godly choices for spending our money and our time. But sometimes we might understand the theory (the why) but not the application (the how). It's time to put these principles from God's Word into practical action. What does it look like to have the proper perspective on our possessions? How do we know when our schedule is in a state that will allow us to focus on what's truly important? What does it look like when our attention is focused in a godly way? What ideal are we aiming for? How will we know when we've arrived?

A Godly Relationship with Our Possessions

I'll begin the transition to the more practical, hands-on section of the book with a description of a healthy relationship with our possessions. While there are no absolutes, and everyone's situation is different, we can draw some helpful generalizations.

- Our possessions are used for godly purposes. They reflect our goal of glorifying God. Our belongings don't interfere with the kind of life we want to live for God; rather, they contribute to it.

- Our belongings are in good condition because we've taken care of them.

- We have enough, but not an excess. In any given category, we've kept only what we need.

- When we look around our home, we feel good about how it looks.

- Given a small amount of time to prepare, we are comfortable bringing guests into our home.

- Floors and furniture surfaces are routinely free of clutter. This gives us space to accomplish tasks and to move about freely.

- Our possessions have a purpose; they aren't just kept indefinitely with no plan to use them.

- When we identify useful items we don't need, we give them to someone who can put them to good use. We have a regular habit of donating unneeded items.

- We realize our possessions ultimately belong to God. If we see another person or group with a need for them, we are able to give them away because we're not emotionally attached to them.

- Our belongings are in good order; we can find what we need easily and quickly.

- Every item has a home, a place where it belongs. Items are kept in their home when not in use. After use, they are returned to their home.

- Our belongings relate to who we are now or the kind of person we want to be, or they remind us of a positive experience in our life. They don't keep us in a part of our past that weighs us down with guilt and shame.

- We love and use everything we own.

- When our schedule is busy or we have an unanticipated change of schedule, our home may temporarily reflect some disorder. However, as soon as the situation changes, we can restore order quickly.

A Godly Relationship with Our Schedule

As we turn from physical possessions to our schedule, obviously we'll need to think more theoretically. It's just as important with this category to make sure we can translate the theory into application. God's Word gives us enduring truths we can use to make decisions about any area of our lives, including how we spend our time.

I've heard many times that you can tell what someone values by the way they spend their time and their money. Developing a godly relationship with our schedule is surely important work. We can't control every aspect of our schedule. For example, if you teach high school, you can't

> You can tell what someone values by the way they spend their time and their money.

start work at 10 a.m. no matter how much you and your students might desire that schedule. And there are many activities that we must make time for whether we enjoy them or not (that yard isn't going to mow itself). Even so, we have control over most of our schedule. We can choose how we spend most of our time. The more we surrender our time to the principles of God's Word, the more He'll be able to use us to glorify Him and to serve others. Living in a way that matches our priorities gives us fulfillment and contentment.

- Our time is used for godly purposes. As believers, the activities that fill our days are in line with the principles of Scripture; in short, our walk matches our talk.

- We prioritize time for Bible study and prayer.

- Recognizing that our time is not our own but belongs to God, if the Holy Spirit speaks to us about a need, we are willing to change our schedule to meet that need.

- We take time to gather in community with other believers, knowing that we need the encouragement and accountability to stay faithful.

- Knowing that our bodies are temples of the Holy Spirit, we take time to keep our bodies healthy with proper nutrition, exercise, good sleep habits, and medical care.

- We are unselfish with our time; we freely give our time to others as we are able.

- We take time for ourselves as needed to make sure we are physically and emotionally equipped to help others.

- When we are presented with a possible activity, we evaluate its merits as it compares to our values. We don't allow guilt to force us to say "yes" to something that either doesn't align with our values or that we can't fit into our schedules.

- We don't fill our schedule so full that we don't have adequate time with our friends and family and adequate time to take care of ourselves.

- We examine our schedule in detail to assure that everything on it has a reason to be there, a purpose that aligns with our beliefs.

- If our schedule gets so full that we feel overwhelmed and we can't devote the necessary time to essential activities, we reevaluate as soon as possible. We eliminate items from our schedule as needed until we achieve a balance that works for us and our family.

A Godly Relationship with Our Attention

What we pay attention to contributes to our thoughts, our actions, and even shapes the direction of our lives. Our brains are incredibly complex organs that contribute to actions as diverse as interpreting the sight of a rainbow, moving our hand away from the hot surface of a stove, and daydreaming during a conference. No one could ever claim the ability to totally control their every thought. However, we have more control over our thoughts than we may think (pun intended). We may not be able to stop a thought from entering our brain, but we can control how long it remains there and what action(s) we take as a result. We control much of what we allow to enter our minds. God's Word teaches us that we certainly have the ability and the responsibility to pay attention to and train our minds.

- We do our best to focus our minds on what is going on at the current moment.

- If we are with other people, we recognize that they are more important than anything else in our surroundings. We pay attention to them and don't allow ourselves to be distracted by our digital devices (phone, tablet, etc.).

- In conversation with others, we listen to them. We don't interrupt their speech or formulate our next words while they are speaking.

- We do our best to keep our mind on godly thoughts.

- When our attention diverts to ungodly topics, we quickly recognize it and take steps to remedy it.

- We are careful about what we allow ourselves to take into our minds through what we read, listen to, or watch.

These lists are not meant to overwhelm or intimidate you, but to give you a mental picture of a goal for which to strive. Just as your clutter in various forms didn't accumulate overnight, reaching this goal won't happen overnight. But with God's power, you can certainly reach it. Chapters 11 and 12 include practical tips to guide you in decluttering for each of these clutter categories.

෨ 10 ෫

What Is the Overall Organizing Process?

A t this point, I hope you're feeling grounded in Scripture and ready to begin taking action. Time spent in Scripture, theory, motivation, and reflection are crucial for success in lifelong change. Change always happens in our minds before it ever gets interpreted into action. You have to understand the why before you start on the how. Not only that, but jumping right into the action before establishing your standards, as tempting as it is, can lead you to quick progress that doesn't last. You want to make changes that last, right? I dare say many of you have made attempts to declutter and organize before, and those attempts may not have led to long-term success. Finally, we're not tossing those scriptural principles aside when we start taking action steps. Those principles will guide us along the way, especially when we encounter obstacles. And we will definitely encounter some obstacles.

We've got one more essential step to take before we dive into decluttering and organizing. Whether I'm advising someone who is working on their own or I'm working together with a client, I always recommend starting with a serious and comprehensive assessment. I ask a lot of questions because in order to effectively help, I have to know their situation well. These questions are also useful for you to consider as you begin the decluttering and organizing process.

For each category of clutter, I'll begin by explaining how to do a thorough assessment. Then I'll briefly explain the overall 3-step organizing process for each category. I'll start with physical clutter first, and then move on to schedule clutter and attention clutter. The overall organizing process is the same for any type of clutter, but the steps will look different depending on the category.

For this chapter, focus on completing a thorough assessment for each category. Then read through the information about the 3-step organizing process so that you understand the entire process. Then in the next chapters we'll start working on decluttering, the first step of the process.

You won't necessarily need to complete such a thorough assessment every time you get ready to organize. But I would still recommend taking some time to at least consider your goals and what is working or not working each time you're preparing to organize. Time spent assessing a situation before taking action is always a valuable use of time.

Assessment of your Physical Clutter

Before answering the following questions about your physical clutter, walk around your home to gauge the level of clutter and disorganization. Take notes as you walk around, then answer these questions:

- What is your overall goal? Describe the ideal outcome for how your home would look and function after decluttering and organizing is complete.

- How will your home and work situation affect your efforts to get organized and to maintain the order?

- Has disorganization and clutter been an issue for most of your life, or has a recent life change contributed to the disorder?

- What has prevented you from successfully getting organized on your own so far?

- What specific problem areas do you see?

- Are there areas of your home in which the current organization works well for you that you can use as a model for other areas?

Three Simple Organizing Steps for Physical Clutter

Armed with a clear picture of the situation and defined goals, it's time to start with the first action. The overall process of organizing can be divided into 3 simple steps:

1. Declutter
2. Arrange
3. Maintain

We'll be dealing predominantly with the decluttering step. However, it's helpful to lay out all of the steps first so you can understand how decluttering fits into the whole process.

These 3 steps work for organizing anything! You can use these steps while organizing a garage, bathroom, closet, or any area of the home. You can use them for organizing digital items like email, spreadsheets, and digital photos. You can even use them for organizing your schedule.

Declutter

The first step in the organizing process is to declutter. Decluttering means getting rid of anything that isn't needed. Decluttering is the most important step of the process. In fact, if you only decluttered and didn't go any further, you would still see huge results in your home.

Although decluttering is the most important and most needed step and should always be accomplished first, it's the step many people skip for several reasons. First, it's a difficult step because you have to make tough choices, which can be mentally taxing. We don't part with our things very easily (one of the many reasons we have clutter in the first place). In addition, many people like to skip decluttering because the second step (arranging) is what most people consider "organizing." Many people (including me!) really enjoy buying organizing containers, trying to pick ones that are just perfect for an area, matching the color and style of the room, etc. The problem with skipping straight to arranging is that without decluttering, all we're doing is shifting our clutter around! I call this practice "stuff shifting," and it isn't an effective method of organizing at all. We'll be going into detail about decluttering our stuff in Chapter 12, "How Do I Declutter My Belongings?".

Arrange

The second step in the organizing process is to arrange. Arranging is admittedly the most enjoyable step of the process for many people. When we arrange, we decide on the best location and type of storage for the items that remain after decluttering is complete. Only after we get rid of what we don't need can we select the ideal location and container because only then will we know how much we have in any given category.

Every item needs to have a home, a location where it stays when it isn't in use. This is the key foundational principle in organizing. Each category of items should have just one home, not multiple locations. Ideally the home should be close to where the item is used. If an item is used by multiple people in the home, each person should weigh in on the decision of where and how to store it.

When an item is removed from its home to be used, it should be replaced in the same location as quickly as possible after its use. There are many other factors involved in choosing the proper home for an item. A few examples include putting the most used items in easy to access areas, making sure any dangerous items are out of the reach of children, considering mobility issues, etc.

When it comes to choosing containers, the possibilities are almost endless. While finding the perfect container is wonderful, frequently we can save money by just using containers we already own, or "shopping at home." If you've done a thorough job during the decluttering process, you will likely have numerous empty containers available.

You don't have to have expensive organizing products for this step. Almost anything will do! Empty shoe boxes make great containers. Dollar stores have plenty of useful options. Of course, if budget isn't an issue or you need a specialty product, there are even more options. Don't get hung up on finding the perfect product. You can always use something less than ideal temporarily while you move on to other areas if you've got lots of decluttering to do.

Maintain

The third step in the organizing process is to maintain the established order. By this stage, all unnecessary items have been removed (decluttering), and locations and containers have been established for every item (arranging). A lot of work has been accomplished, and the home looks fantastic. Step back, admire the progress, and celebrate!

But before your celebration goes too far, you've got to figure out a plan to keep things in order. This is probably the most difficult step of the process. In order for maintenance to be truly successful, it should be in the forefront of your mind before you even begin the step of arranging. If you've set up an organizing system that can't be effectively maintained, you've probably wasted your time, and you're going to end up frustrated. Here's a great example.

Suppose parents want to create an organizing system in a children's playroom for all of their LEGO® bricks. There are so many options for organizing bricks (color, shape, size, set, etc.). Suppose the parents decide the bricks should be kept in multiple containers and arranged by color. They spend hours putting all of the red bricks in one container, all of the blue in another, and so on and labeling all of the containers.

Although sorting bricks by color is a valid way to group them, this system might not last too long. If the children who play with them are like most, the first time they play with them, they will probably dump them all out and mix them all together. Probably none of the children would want to take the time to separate them by color again and replace them into the containers.

Instead, consider this strategy: Get the children together and talk about the problem and potential solutions. Ask them what kind of organizing system would be most helpful for them to find what they need while playing with their bricks. Consider several options and talk about whether they would be able to replace them in that arrangement after playing. Pick the best overall solution and try it for a while. If it's not working, you might need to try something else. Keep going until you find the best arrangement.

I often have to rearrange areas several times before finding the ideal organizing system, even in my own home. I frequently tell clients that if the system I helped them set up doesn't work for them, I want them to tell me so they (or we) can adjust it until it works. After discussing all of the alternatives and considering all of the factors and people involved, arranging and maintaining can still be a process of trial and error.

Even with the ideal organizing system and our best efforts, there's no guarantee that order will be maintained long-term. No home can stay perfectly organized at all times. Normal day-to-day life creates some disorder, and during busier seasons like the holidays, the tendency towards disorder is accentuated. The true measure of a space's level of organization is how quickly order can be reestablished after it is disturbed.

Consider these examples: Your office is normally well organized. The floor and desk are usually clear, drawers aren't too stuffed with belongings, and file folders are neat and alphabetical. You are tasked with a huge project that requires you to neglect the maintenance of your office organization for a period of time. By the end of the project, your office looks like a tornado has swept through it. When the project is completed, it only takes about an hour to get the room back in shape. Your office is definitely an organized space because order was reestablished very quickly.

> The true measure of a space's level of organization is how quickly order can be reestablished after it is disturbed.

Imagine the same situation in a different office. There are a few piles of paper on the desk, the drawers are a jumbled mess of office supplies, and the files are in random order. The office owner begins the huge project, and any organization the office might have had is destroyed. When the project is completed, it might take this person half a day or more to get the office in order. Because the office wasn't very organized to begin with, they can't just quickly return items to their proper home and move on. They'll need to clean up the mess from the project as well as establishing order to the entire space.

When disorder and backsliding occur, catch it early, get the area back into order, and move on. While you can learn from the situation and improve next time, it does no good to berate yourself over it. Figure out what led to the problem and what changes can be made to prevent the same situation in the future.

Sometimes it's helpful to set up a schedule for maintenance of problem areas. Paper and digital document organizing are two examples from my own home. I have one container for paper that comes into the house, and I go through it once a week. This prevents it from piling up and prevents me from forgetting appointments, bills, events, etc. I go through my digital documents twice a year, usually in the summer and during the holidays. This helps me prevent digital clutter.

I helped a client create a maintenance schedule for the part of her basement where household tools were stored. Although the area had been organized at times in the past, maintenance of the order had proved difficult to impossible. The main problem was that when a set of tools was removed for a project, the tools were often placed in random spots instead of being returned to their proper locations. If the tools were taken out of the area in a container, the container of tools was set somewhere temporarily but the tools were never removed and put back in their homes.

In an ideal world, as soon as you finish using something, you should return it to its home immediately. We all know we don't live in an ideal world. Sometimes when we finish a project, there simply isn't time to return the items. We may be too tired or distracted by other things. For whatever reason, the ideal isn't realized, and disorder results.

When this is a consistent problem in a particular area, instead of beating yourself up about it or constantly nagging someone who's not following the plan, it's sometimes helpful to set up a system. I instructed my client to create a drop zone, or an area where tools could be placed temporarily until an opportunity arose to put them back where they belong. She and her husband established an empty bin on an empty shelf as the drop zone. When there is free time or when that bin fills up, items can be returned. If someone is looking for a tool that isn't in its home, now, instead of looking literally everywhere, they can just look in the drop zone. Simple systems for maintenance can do wonders for keeping order.

Assessment of your Schedule Clutter

As we change our focus from physical clutter to schedule clutter and attention clutter, we're going to be turning from working with physical items to more theoretical thinking. We'll need to switch to more 'big picture' and philosophical reasoning. The basic concepts are the same, and the scriptural foundations are just as applicable.

Here are some questions to ask yourself as you assess your level of schedule clutter:

- What is your overall goal? Describe the ideal outcome for what your schedule would look like after decluttering and organizing is complete.

- Do you regularly make time in your schedule for Bible study and prayer? If not, what would be the best way to build this routine into your schedule?

- Do you feel good about the amount of time you devote to your family? Do your family members complain you don't have enough time for them?

- Are you satisfied with the amount of time you devote to your friends? Do your friends complain that you don't have enough time for them?

- How much margin (unscheduled/free time) would you like so that you have sufficient time to relax and time to be available for impromptu opportunities or needs?

- How will your home and work situation affect your choices in organizing and maintaining your schedule?

- Has a cluttered schedule been an issue for most of your life, or has a recent life change or your current stage of life made it more of an issue?

- What has prevented you from successfully addressing your cluttered schedule on your own so far?

- Do you feel pressure to stay at a certain level of busyness based on busy people around you?

- Do you feel more successful or better about yourself when your schedule is full?

- What specific problem areas do you see in your schedule? What problem areas do your family or your friends see?

- Can you think back to a time in your life when your schedule was at an ideal level of activity? If so, can you use this as a model for your current schedule?

Three Simple Organizing Steps for Schedule Clutter

Declutter

The first step in the organizing process is always to declutter. Decluttering means getting rid of anything that isn't needed. When it comes to our schedule, decluttering will mean getting rid of either regular or occasional activities that aren't good choices for us or for our family. Just like with physical clutter, this stage of letting go is the most difficult one.

If an activity has been on your calendar for a long time, it may feel wrong to let it go. If you are a person who has trouble saying "no" or if you have a high level of responsibility, you may feel guilty dropping volunteer activities from your schedule. Guilt can be a strong motivator, but it isn't a good enough motivator to keep a commitment on our calendar if it's not serving us well.

I'm not suggesting you suddenly drop every commitment and leave a person or group in a difficult predicament. But I am suggesting you examine your schedule with a critical eye. We'll be going into great detail about decluttering our schedule in Chapter 11, "How Do I Declutter My Schedule and My Mind?".

Arrange

The second step in the overall organizing process is arranging. When we arrange, we decide on the best location for items that remain after decluttering is complete. When discussing schedule clutter, we're not arranging physical items; we're arranging activities. We've gotten rid of everything in our schedule that doesn't serve us well now, and we're deciding when and how we'll fit in the activities we want to include. Some activities by their very nature have a fixed "place" in our calendar. If an activity is scheduled for a particular day and time, we can't just shuffle it to where it fits best on our personal calendar. Our every other Wednesday evening church Small Group already has a set place on our calendar. A Thursday lunch networking meeting has a set place as well.

We have a host of tasks to schedule which can be accomplished at more flexible times. If we want to make time for exercise, depending on what kind of exercise and where we practice it, we can fit it in at various spots in our schedule. The same holds true for hobbies like reading, crafts, or practicing a musical instrument. Spending time in Bible study, prayer, or serving others is somewhat flexible as well. The same holds true for staying connected with family and friends.

In essence, what we're talking about when we arrange our schedule is time management. Once we've decided on the activities that are important to us (and have decluttered the rest), we now have to figure out how to fit these activities into a schedule that is healthy for us and for those we love. Of all the things in our life that require organizing, I believe organizing our time is the most significant of all!

> **Organizing our time is the most significant of all!**

Usually when we talk about time management, we're interested in how to get more accomplished. Productivity at work or home is important. Anyone who knows me at all knows I love figuring out ways to be more productive.

But wise and godly time management is much more profound.

If we want to manage our time in a godly way, we need to make sure we're spending our time in a way that pleases God. The Scripture is clear in advising us to concentrate our efforts on loving God and loving others. If we're the most productive person in the world but the way we use our time doesn't prioritize loving God or loving others, it's all for naught. We've successfully gotten a lot accomplished, but we picked the wrong work. We need to focus more on the "what" than the "how" by choosing to do what's best in God's eyes.

Maintain

Once you've adjusted your schedule to include all of the activities you want and that are healthy for you, the final challenge is to maintain the schedule. Maintaining the schedule exactly isn't realistic. Schedule changes are a normal part of life. Hopefully you'll find the "sweet spot" with your schedule where you have just the right amount of your time scheduled but not too much.

Once you've ascertained that level, commit yourself to a one in, one out policy with your schedule. Don't add an activity until you remove another. When you are presented with an opportunity to add another event to your calendar or a task to your To-Do list, force yourself to find an event or task to remove. It may not be on the same day or a similar task, but it will still lighten the overall load. I use this one in, one out strategy with physical items, as well. If you're an overachiever and tend to overcommit yourself, you'll be tempted to let more things creep onto your calendar. Don't do it!

How do you stick to this decision to not overcommit? Employing a one in, one out strategy is a good first step, but it's likely you'll need more strategies to ensure success. Another strategy I recommend is to get a "NO!" Mentor. In Episode 21 of Emily P. Freeman's podcast *The Next Right Thing*[20], Emily describes the importance of her sister Miquyllin's input in her life. Miquyllin acts as Emily's *"NO!"* Mentor. She knows Emily so well that she is a good judge of what is in Emily's best interest. So when Emily is presented with a new opportunity, she asks for her sister's advice. Sometimes the new opportunity is exactly what she needs, and she and her sister agree that saying "yes" is the best choice. But other times, Emily knows she should say, "no", but she lacks the courage.

We all need a good "NO!" Mentor, especially if saying "no" isn't easy. You might have guessed that my husband Eric is my "NO!" Mentor. He does such a good job helping me with these kinds of decisions, and I ask his opinion over and over again. Believe it or not, I am getting better at saying "no," and sometimes I serve as my own "NO!" Mentor. As we mature and learn more about what puts us over our limits, we can make better choices with our time.

If you have a tendency for too much leisure time or have trouble with self-discipline, you'll be tempted to start omitting things like Bible study and exercise. Add in some accountability if you need it. Sometimes just publicly stating our intentions is a small form of accountability. You could join a Bible study group or just ask a friend to join you in a Bible study and pledge to ask each other how it's going. You could take part in a group exercise class or walk, bike, or hike with a friend. Go back to your priorities and the Scripture.

Maintaining our habits is the step everyone dreads because it's the toughest one. In thinking back on my life, I am certain I have avoided changes I knew I desperately needed to make because I was afraid I wouldn't be able to maintain the changes. I recall several times when I felt moved to start a regular Bible study or prayer routine. Because I had tried many times before and eventually fallen by the wayside, I was afraid to try again. I didn't want to face the disappointment and sense of failure. And I didn't want to disappoint God.

That posture of fear and cycle of inconsistency is a sign of being human! Only Jesus could confidently claim perfection in his walk with God. Each time we struggle in keeping up our good habits, God welcomes us back with open arms. We can't let our fear of failure keep us from taking action.

We have the unconditional love of our Father and the Spirit of the Almighty God inside us to give us strength! Here is some inspiration:

> For God has not given us a spirit of fear and timidity, but of power, love, and self-discipline.
>
> II Timothy 1:7 (NLT)

Assessment of your Attention Clutter

Assessing and organizing when it comes to attention clutter is the most theoretical of all. After all, we're talking about neither physical items nor events on our calendar. We're talking about what our minds are focused on. In Chapter 3, I defined attention clutter as "the way our minds are constantly absent from the here and now. It's a lack of focus, a lack of ability to concentrate on the person or task at hand, not being 'in the moment'." We'll need to look for more subtle evidence of this type of clutter in our assessment and be open to some inventive approaches to combat it.

To determine your level of attention clutter, consider these questions:

- How often do people complain that you're not listening to them?

- Do you find that even though you have heard someone's words, you still need to ask them to repeat themselves?

- Do you miss the last part of what a person says because you're already formulating your answer before they finish speaking?

- Do you frequently lose items?

- Are you often late to appointments or do you miss them completely because your mind is elsewhere?

- How many hours of a typical day do you spend looking at some kind of a screen at something unrelated to your work, to a project you are working on, or to correspondence with a loved one?

- Is checking your smartphone the last thing you do before you go to sleep and the first thing you do when you wake up?

- Do you use your smartphone while at the table with family or friends?

- Do the notifications on your smartphone usually prompt you to take action regardless of who you're with or what you're doing at the time?

- Do friends and family members complain that you're on your smartphone too much?

Three Simple Organizing Steps for Attention Clutter

Declutter

Attention clutter is sometimes called mental clutter because it's predominantly concerned with our minds. Just the thought of trying to control our thoughts is kind of intimidating. But just because it's difficult doesn't mean it can't or shouldn't be attempted. In fact, the Bible reminds us to watch our thought life.

> Do not conform to the pattern of this world, but be transformed by the renewing of your mind. Then you will be able to test and approve what God's will is—his good, pleasing and perfect will.
>
> Romans 12:2 (NIV)

We may not have complete control over every thought, but we have more control than we may realize. When our thoughts drift into inappropriate content, we choose how long we allow ourselves to stay in those thoughts. We can choose to move on to more worthy subjects.

What kinds of attention and thoughts do we need to declutter? Basically, we need to get rid of any thoughts that draw us away from God. Thoughts that are negative, complaining, and focused on what's wrong with our lives are

> We need to get rid of any thoughts that draw us away from God.

obvious candidates for decluttering, as are judgmental thoughts about others and how they aren't measuring up to some standard. Endlessly worrying about every scenario that could go wrong leads us further from God.

Don't forget to consider the way you think about yourself. Sometimes when we make a mistake, we say things to ourselves that we would never dream of saying to a friend. Things like: "You're so stupid!" "It's no wonder no one wants to be your friend!" "You'll never be able to change that!" This kind of negative self-talk is one of your worst enemies.

God does not speak to us this way. He may very well call us out on a sinful behavior that we need to change, but He does so in love. He speaks to us as his precious sons and daughters. He builds us up and encourages us to keep going. He restores our soul.

When you catch yourself dwelling in negative thoughts about others, the world, your life, or yourself, catch yourself quickly. Don't dwell on them. Bring yourself back to God and His Word.

> The weapons we fight with are not the weapons of the world. On the contrary, they have divine power to demolish strongholds. We demolish arguments and every pretension that

> sets itself up against the knowledge of God, and
> we take captive every thought to make it obedient
> to Christ.
>
> II Corinthians 10:4–5 (NIV)

When we realize our minds are drifting and we're not fully invested in the people and circumstances around us, we can take steps to get back to the present. It's not easy. It's going to take some training. I've got a long way to go on this one. You'll find techniques and ideas in the next chapter to help you.

Arrange

To a large extent, we choose the majority of what we consume with our minds. We choose the content and amount of what we read, what we watch, and what we listen to. We choose how much time we spend on our devices. We choose what we feed our minds.

We can consciously and deliberately choose to feed our minds with good food. We can and must nourish our minds, hearts, and souls with God's Word. There is no better fuel for our spirits.

> And the peace of God, which transcends all
> understanding, will guard your hearts and your
> minds in Christ Jesus. Finally, brothers and sisters,
> whatever is true, whatever is noble, whatever is
> right, whatever is pure, whatever is lovely,
> whatever is admirable—if anything is excellent or
> praiseworthy—think about such things.
>
> Philippians 4:7–8 (NIV)

Consider Jesus' words as He was being tested by Satan in the desert:

> Jesus answered, 'It is written: "Man shall not live on bread alone, but on every word that comes from the mouth of God."'
>
> Matthew 4:4 (NIV)

We can also feed our spirits with wholesome music, books, podcasts, Bible teaching, etc. I'm not implying we must spend every waking moment on purely spiritual content. Nor am I preaching against any particular choices of entertainment. I'm not here to judge. But we must be more intentional with what we allow ourselves to consume.

Maintain

As Christians, we are in the midst of spiritual warfare. If we're not aware that we're in a war, we're undoubtedly losing the fight. Satan knows our weaknesses. He will aim first to change the way we think about God and will tempt us to question God's goodness. Guarding our thoughts and keeping a spiritual perspective are essential to living a godly life. I don't say this to intimidate or alarm but to persuade us to take this seriously.

How do we guard our thoughts? Let's look again at the passage from Philippians 4 for a little more context.

> Do not be anxious about anything, but in every situation, by prayer and petition, with thanksgiving, present your requests to God. And the peace of God, which transcends all understanding, will guard your hearts and your minds in Christ Jesus. Finally, brothers and sisters, whatever is true, whatever is noble, whatever is right, whatever is pure, whatever is lovely, whatever is admirable—if anything is excellent or praiseworthy—think about such things. Whatever you have learned or

received or heard from me, or seen in me—put it into practice. And the God of peace will be with you.

Philippians 4:6–9 (NIV)

Yes, we have a formidable battle on our hands. But we also have the truth in God's Word to guide us. And we have the Lord Himself on our side. We are truly set up to win.

Now that you know the three basic steps of the overall organizing process (declutter, arrange, and maintain), we're going to turn our attention to decluttering.

ೞ 11 ೕ

How Do I Declutter My Schedule and My Mind?

It's time to get started with some concrete actions to deal with our clutter. I know some of you are thinking, "Finally! I thought we'd never get to this part of the book!" Fair enough. I hear you. If we don't take time to assess, to gain a godly understanding, and to establish a clear direction, we might as well be building our house on the sand. Remember the story of the wise and foolish builders from Matthew 7? Building on God's Word (the rock) works so much better than building on sand! We're going to start with decluttering solutions for the most prevalent and insidious kinds of clutter, schedule clutter and attention clutter.

Decluttering your schedule and attention first will give you more time to work on your physical clutter. Your decluttered mind will be freed to consider what choices will best serve others and glorify God. You'll have the proper perspective to make the best choices about your possessions.

Schedule Clutter

Recall our discussion in Chapter 3 concerning today's culture as the culture of the busy, where a packed calendar is commonplace and sometimes even regarded as a virtue. Years ago, my life was a prime example of an overambitious person with a cluttered schedule deep in the throes of the culture of the busy. I am not alone in this struggle. Many of my friends and clients are dealing with these same issues.

I have used the following measures myself and with clients to help them alleviate the problem of schedule clutter. While all of us have our own unique situations, the general principles of these strategies are applicable for anyone. A decluttered schedule and a heart to follow the Spirit's lead will give you so many opportunities to glorify God.

Clearly Define your Priorities

Spend some time thinking about what you value. This is a task best done in a relaxed setting with just you and God. Include Bible study and prayer in this time. A schedule that doesn't align with your priorities should raise a warning flag in your mind. You need to correct the disparity between the two immediately.

We don't want to be the kind of person who says that serving God is the most important thing in their life but doesn't ever spend time serving others, praying, studying the Bible, etc. We also don't want to be the kind of person who says spending time with their family is very important but who rarely take the time to actually do that or does it reluctantly because they'd rather get things accomplished. Saying one thing but doing another, or pretending to be something we're not, is the very definition of hypocrisy. If we're willing to be honest with ourselves, we may see areas of hypocrisy in our own lives.

It's so easy to "talk the talk" but not "walk the walk." It's so easy to flippantly use the "I don't have time" excuse. The reality is we make time for what we consider most important. We figure out a way to make it work in our schedule. At more challenging times in our lives such as parenting young children, times of sickness, or the loss of a loved one, we may not have as much time as we wish. But we all can and must make time for what we value.

> We must make time for what we value.

I have had seasons of my life where my schedule didn't match my priorities. I have been there and done that, and I don't ever want to go back. I refuse to let things of lesser importance keep me from making time with God and with my family a priority.

Establish Clear Boundaries

Limit work time to defined work hours so you can be fully present at home. For some jobs, this isn't much of a struggle because our work hours are clearly delineated. Many jobs require being at a particular location for the work, and overtime isn't possible or even allowed. However, especially in this day and age where so much remote work is possible, especially with answering emails and working on digital documents, the boundaries can blur. When we constantly check emails and texts on our devices, it's tempting to jump right back into work during our home time.

In my situation, as a new business owner who LOVES her job, I hardly ever want to stop working. I can always find one more task to complete or one more idea to explore. Add in a splash of perfectionism, drive, and competitiveness, and you've got a recipe for a workaholic. I didn't even realize how many hours I was working until, you guessed it, Eric brought it to my attention. It was eye-opening to admit I was working far more hours than I had intended and that my business was occupying too large a part of my life.

I had to establish some clear boundaries. I don't work on my business in the evenings or on weekends unless a particular client can only schedule appointments during those hours. If I have to work evenings or weekends, if possible, I schedule it during a time when Eric has another commitment. This boundary hasn't been too difficult. But I still struggle with the boundary of not dealing with work email or phone calls outside of work hours. When I go outside this boundary, I am not able to give my full attention to whatever I'm doing or the people with whom I am interacting. Smartphones make slipping back into the habit so easy.

Learn from my mistakes and don't let this happen to you. If you're in this situation already, own up to it, confess it, and commit to changing it. Your family deserves your full attention.

Evaluate Every Calendar Commitment

Take a hard look at every regular commitment on your calendar. Just because you have always committed to Obligation A, enjoyed it, are very good at it, and other people are relying on you to do it, doesn't mean you need to commit to Obligation A forever. You know how it is—you agree to be on some sort of committee, and because there is no established "exit strategy," the unspoken understanding is you will be on that committee forever. Even then, you are subtly expected to "replace yourself" should you decide to leave. For those of us who pride ourselves on reliability, the pressure is real.

It all goes back to our priorities and our purpose. Evaluate your calendar against your priorities. Let's say two of your top priorities are to help people see Jesus through your words and your actions and to spend plenty of quality time with your family. Look at each item on your calendar and ask yourself, "Does this activity show people Jesus? Can others see Jesus in the way I participate in this activity? Does this activity involve spending time with my family? If not, does participating in this activity still leave me with plenty of time for my family?" You can also use the questions in Chapter 10 in the section "Assessment of Your Schedule Clutter" as a guide.

Say "Yes" to Less

Start saying yes to less. If you are like me and have a terrible time saying "No," this won't be easy. But it's absolutely essential. You've probably heard that when you say "yes" to one thing, you're saying "no" to something else. It's really true! If our schedule is so full that we don't have any margins in it, that's a setup for stress.

Swallow your pride and have an earnest conversation with your family about how you spend your time. It doesn't mean you need to let your family control your schedule. Your schedule is your decision. Nevertheless, we don't always see clearly how our decisions affect those we love.

This example may help you understand the dilemma. I have a client who loves to serve, and she is often asked to volunteer in community groups. She enjoys the work immensely and has a real talent for it. But every time she accepts an offer to volunteer, especially for a big project, it takes time away from her efforts to organize her own home and from time with her family. Her family members are sometimes frustrated that she agrees to help so often because it means that she will be gone more often than they like and that she will be anxious and overwhelmed, which affects her mood at home. She feels guilty turning down opportunities because the groups are doing such great work. She is finally learning that in order to have time with her family and to be her best self at home, she needs to limit her volunteer activity.

Take Time for Yourself

Spend some time thinking about what relaxes you and what makes you happy. Figure out how to work those activities into your schedule. What do you get really excited about doing? If you had a Saturday all to yourself and could spend it doing anything you want to do, what would you choose? It could be a hobby you've not participated in for years or something as simple as walking in the neighborhood and listening to music. Whatever it is, if at all possible, figure out a way to make it work. Taking time to relax is good for us. When we take time for ourselves, we are better fueled to give to others.

One such activity I identified is reading for pleasure. I have always loved to read; I find it enjoyable, relaxing, and educational. Sadly, I realized I had gotten so busy I wasn't reading for pleasure anymore. Lightening my load and rejoining a book club have helped me bring reading for pleasure back into my life.

Are you willing to take a hard look at how you spend your time? Are you open to your family and friends' input? Everyone's life situation is unique, so your conclusions and remedies won't be the same as your best friend's; they will need to fit your life. I can guarantee time spent in reflection and the decisions that come from that reflection will be well worth it.

Attention Clutter

In Chapter 3, we defined attention clutter, also called mental clutter, as an inability to focus on what is going on around us. Our body is present in the situation, but our mind is somewhere completely different. When we struggle with attention clutter, we may be physically in the middle of a meaningful conversation with a friend, but mentally, we are pondering the events on tomorrow's agenda or figuring out which items on our To-Do list we will tackle next.

Many different factors contribute to attention clutter. In my own life, the number one factor by a landslide is my smartphone. Do you remember the alarming statistics I shared in Chapter 3? One of the most remarkable devices ever invented can become one of the most destructive devices ever in the hands of a person with attention clutter. This was so true for me. It's an ongoing issue I suppose I will always have to fight. The measures I have taken have helped tremendously, and they have helped my clients as well. The following strategies can be applied to smartphones as well as tablets and computers.

Strategies for your Smartphone

Don't Use your Smartphone During Mealtime

There are occasionally situations where an exception can be made to the rule, but for the most part, it's a better choice to keep your smartphone out of the dinnertime gathering. Our best conversations typically transpire over a table. Conversation with the people at the table should have priority, whether we're at home or eating out. If you're eating out, you might consider leaving your smartphone in the car to avoid the temptation altogether.

Since I started getting a handle on my smartphone addiction, I am even more aware of how widespread the problem is in our culture. Again, this applies to people of all ages. When you're eating in a restaurant, have you noticed how often you see families sitting at the table but not talking at all? Some or all of them are staring intently at their smartphone screens. Have you seen parents on their phones while the children are just sitting there eating? How about couples out together with either one or both of them on their phones? Again, sometimes there are legitimate reasons for being on our phones. But most of the time, whatever we're doing can wait. The people at the table are the priority.

Limit Smartphone Use as a Car Passenger

As a driver, avoiding smartphone use is a matter of life and death. But as a passenger, it's all too easy to use travel time as a reason to get on our smartphone. This subtly communicates to the driver and any other passengers that whatever you're doing on the phone is the most important thing going on. A better choice is to choose something everyone can participate in. Try listening to a book or a podcast together. Better yet, how about just looking out the window and observing what's going on around you?

Charge Your Smartphone Away from your Bedside

Having your smartphone right beside you is definitely convenient. Be that as it may, convenience isn't always the most important factor. With our phone right beside us, we are much more likely to spend time on it late into the night and in the middle of the night, as well as hopping right back on it first thing in the morning. Try moving it across the room and see how it changes your habits.

This small adjustment has reaped big dividends for me, and I highly recommend you try it. Instead of checking my email or scrolling through social media before I go to sleep, I'm reading a novel or talking to my husband. I no longer look at my phone if I happen to wake up during the night. I don't check my phone first thing in the morning as often as I used to; in fact, occasionally I don't even look at it for several hours after I'm awake.

I honestly had never thought about changing my charging location until I heard a sermon by Trevor Atwood called "The King's Clock: How the Sabbath Shapes our Time and Money" at City Church in Murfreesboro, Tennessee.[21] I learned in this sermon that clocks were originally created by monks as reminders to pray. We tend to use our phones as our clocks now. Isn't it ironic that the device invented by monks to bring us closer to God is now leading us further away and, in a sense, becoming our god?

Limit your Social Media Time

Spending time on Facebook, Instagram, LinkedIn, and other social media platforms is not wrong. Tools like these can be excellent ways to stay in touch with friends and family members we rarely see. But if we're honest with ourselves, most of our social media time is wasted idle time. Again, it's ok to spend some time this way. However, if we're not careful we will find ourselves spending much more time on social media than we intend to and more time than is mentally healthy for us.

In order to decrease your social media time, it may be helpful to identify the reason(s) you spend so much time on it. Your desire may be tied to FOMO (Fear of Missing Out) as it was (and still is) for me. FOMO is defined as "the worry that one may miss an enjoyable activity, especially due to the fact that one often sees others documenting such activities on social media."[22] We want to keep up with "the latest" news on people's lives, and we don't want to miss an opportunity to participate in an enjoyable event. Or it might just be a desire for mindless entertainment. Identifying your "why" can help because you may realize your reasons aren't that important. You may think of better ways to accomplish the same purpose.

I tried some halfhearted efforts to curb my social media addiction. Much like a smoker trying unsuccessfully to quit smoking, I tried to cut back. But when I finally got serious about conquering this addiction, I had to take more drastic measures. I had to go "cold turkey" by deleting my personal account as well as the Facebook app. It was a big moment for me. When I contemplated deleting the app, I expected to feel a sense of panic, or at the least, remorse. In truth, I breathed a sigh of relief and felt like a burden had been lifted. Please don't misunderstand me. Being on Facebook (or any social media platform) is not wrong. Plenty of people spend a reasonable amount of time on it and use it for the best of purposes. I only know that for me, Facebook had become too consuming in my life, and the only way I could solve the problem was to disconnect.

What about you? How much time do you spend on social media? Have you ever checked? Because smartphone addiction is such a big issue now, mobile phone operating system manufacturers like Apple and Google are including tools to help you monitor and manage your usage. An example of this technology is Screen Time, a tool included on Apple devices running an operating system of iOS 9 or higher. You can see in detail how much time you're spending on all of your devices on texting, phone calls, websites, and particular apps. If you're an Android user, you'll need to use a third-party app like Usage Time or Google's Digital Wellbeing to find this information. If you have Android 9 or 10, you may have Digital Wellbeing in your Settings already. When you find out how much time you're spending on your smartphone, you may find the results eye-opening.

Strategies for Other Distractions

There are many other factors contributing to attention clutter besides smartphone addiction. When we're not mentally present in a situation, it's not always because we're glued to our devices. We could be distracted by a myriad of concerns. We could be mulling over something as trivial as what shirt to wear tomorrow or as weighty as the meaning of life. No matter what the distraction is, it's keeping us from being present in the moment. It's unrealistic to think we could be 100% focused on the present moment 100% of the time. It's healthy and normal to spend some time reflecting on the past and looking forward to the future. But clearly, we should focus the majority of our attention on the present. We can't actively participate in what's going on if we're not mentally and emotionally there.

Some of the tools for increasing mindfulness that have been helpful for me and for my clients include spending time in nature, meditation, counseling, and yoga. I'm trying to be a better listener and to be less self-focused. When I realize my mind is drifting, I try to catch it quickly and get back to the present. I ask more questions to clarify what the speaker is saying and to get to know more about them. I try to resist the urge to fill every second of silence with my own voice. It's a journey I imagine I'll always be taking.

How are you doing with mindfulness? Do you have trouble staying in the present moment? I encourage you to spend some time reflecting on these questions. Ask your family and close friends if they think this is an issue for you (and be open to their honest answers). Research all of the available resources and try some of them. Our mental and emotional health is an essential component of our overall health.

❧ 12 ☙

How Do I Declutter My Belongings?

A re you ready to get started decluttering? If you haven't taken the time to answer the questions in Chapter 10, page 83, do so now before you proceed. Taking time to assess your situation completely and to set goals is invaluable for assuring your success. Go back and take some time to walk around the house and answer these questions, then come back to this chapter.

Ok, NOW are you ready to start? It's completely normal to feel overwhelmed at this point. You may have any or all of the following thoughts:

- "I can't believe I let the clutter get this bad!"

- "This is impossible!"

- "I've done this before but it didn't last. Why will this time be any different?"

- "This is probably the worst clutter on my street/in this neighborhood/in town/in the state/in the country/in the world!"

- "I'll never get a handle on this. Why should I even try?"

- "Help! I have no idea where to start!"

Don't let these thoughts stop you before you even get started! Acknowledge them and move on. Keep your goals in mind throughout the process. You may even want to post your goals somewhere where you can see them regularly, either physically or digitally. Recall the Scriptures about the abundant life God has in mind for you, and look forward. If you live with others, enlist their help with each step of the process. Start with a family meeting to discuss the plan. The more everyone is involved in the process throughout, the better the possibility of success. If you live alone, you might consider asking a friend or family member to go through the journey with you, whether as an encourager or a fellow participant.

Without a doubt, the most difficult part of any big project is just getting started. Once you get over the hump at the beginning and start seeing progress, no matter how small, you'll be motivated to continue. Success breeds success.

The decluttering process can be done in so many different ways, at virtually any pace. Even if you only have the time and/or stamina to work on it for 15 minutes at a time a few days a week, you'll still make progress. I've provided plenty of practical tips you can accomplish in small segments of time. If you'd rather get the work done more quickly and are able to devote large chunks of time to it, that's wonderful. But you can definitely break it into very small sections and still accomplish your goals.

Keep in mind that decluttering isn't just a one-time process; it's a lifestyle change. If you clear every bit of clutter from your home but don't make permanent

> # Decluttering isn't just a one-time process; it's a lifestyle change.

changes in your daily habits, you'll eventually wind up in the same shape somewhere down the road. I'll discuss this in more detail in Chapter 14, "How Do I Prevent Future Clutter?".

With all of these caveats in mind, let's get busy!

Where Should I Start?

If we asked 10 professional organizers this question, we might get 10 different answers. While most organizers have a suggested order we believe is most efficient or that we prefer, just like anything, there is no one right method for everyone. Ultimately, the decision is yours. As long as you continue to make progress, you can start pretty much anywhere! Here are a few options to consider when choosing where to start:

- Daily Routines
- Driving You Crazy
- Door and Commons
- Start Somewhere
- Don't Wait Too Late

Deal with the Daily Routines First

Establishing and maintaining effective daily routines is indispensable for staying organized. Lack of daily routines is a very frequent source of clutter. Without effective routines, piles of dishes, laundry, and random items clutter surfaces. Without those routines, it's just a matter of time before a recently decluttered space is right back in the same mess, maybe even worse. Our daily habits are the real drivers of change, not our occasional frenzied bursts of activity.

> Our daily habits are the real drivers of change.

If you focus on routines and get them down to a science, you're more likely to find the time for more extensive decluttering and organizing projects. Let me explain how this works in a home environment. Let's say you have a big goal of decluttering and organizing a large storage area such as your basement. However, you can't seem to ever catch up on your dishes and laundry, and you have piles of random clutter covering most of your horizontal surfaces. Any free time you have for organizing tends to be spent on dishes, laundry, and cluttered surfaces, so you can't imagine when you'll ever have time to tackle larger projects. The best use of your time is to get those daily tasks under control first by establishing a routine that works for you and can be maintained. Then you can work on finding a block of time to start decluttering and organizing your storage area.

If your daily routines are well established and you have a solid routine for keeping up with them, you may be ready to consider another starting point. Before you make that decision, read through the section on daily routines and ask yourself these questions: Are all of your daily routines working for you? Are they bothering you? Could your daily routines be improved? Are you spending so much time keeping up with daily routines that you don't really have time to do any other organizing tasks?

In terms of daily tasks, focus initially on routines for dishes, laundry, and daily pickup. For each of these, you will have to figure out what works best for you and your schedule. It is more important to *have* a routine than it is to choose a *particular* routine. Just like anything in life, repetition creates habits, and after a certain point, habits become the new normal. There will occasionally be times when the routine can't be kept up for some reason. But if you can get back into the routine quickly, you can prevent backsliding from going too far.

Dishes

When it comes to dishes, this principle applies whether or not you have a dishwasher. You need to choose the best daily time to load the dishwasher (or to wash the dishes in the sink) and to unload the dishwasher (or put up the hand-washed dishes). If you don't do this on a daily basis and the dishes pile up, it takes so much longer to get them under control. I prefer to wash dishes every night and put them up every morning, but this might not be the best schedule for you. Don't make the mistake of using your dish drainer as a storage spot for clean dishes. Get into the habit of emptying it regularly just like the dishwasher. If every dish and utensil in your kitchen has a proper home, putting things away doesn't take long.

Laundry

There are many different types of laundry routines. Some people like doing a load of laundry every day to keep it under control. Some have a regular laundry day once a week or so where they stay at home and tackle it all at once. My laundry routine is to do laundry when the laundry basket gets up to a certain level, which usually happens about twice a week. The biggest mistake people make with laundry is they don't take the time to fold, hang up, and put up the clean laundry quickly after the clothes are finished washing and drying. Before you know it, there is a small mountain taking up valuable space somewhere, and you're faced with wrinkled clothes requiring additional time above the normal routine. It takes much less time to take care of each load as it finishes up than it does to wait until you have multiple loads in a big pile. One method I use to force myself to put laundry up is to fold it on the bed. Before we get into bed at night, we have to move the clothes anyway. Why not take the time to put them away instead of just moving the folded clothes somewhere else?

Daily Pickup

Daily pickup is a crucial routine. I am always amazed at how big a difference it makes to simply clean up after yourself on a regular basis! If you get something out to use it, take a moment and put it back when you're finished. When you return from a shopping trip, put away your purchases immediately. After a trip, if at all possible, unpack immediately. Leave an open block of time in your schedule after you return from a trip for unpacking and getting back into your routines. These simple steps can go a long way towards keeping you organized.

The whole family can get involved in daily pickup. Gather everyone together and set a timer for five minutes. Instruct everyone to look for any trash, items for donation, or anything that needs to be returned to its home. You can make it fun by playing upbeat music or by introducing a little competition. See who can put up the most items or whose room has the least number of items out of place. The more frequently you conduct a five-minute pickup, the more adept everyone will get in the practice. Maybe everyone will get so used to it they won't even complain about it anymore. Perhaps the rest of the family will even initiate it occasionally. It's a lofty goal, but we can all dream.

Driving You Crazy

Start with the Easy Stuff

Start with something you've been looking at for months and thinking, "I really need to get rid of that." You get bonus points if it includes items taking up a large amount of space. It's uncanny how much better a room looks when unneeded bulky items are removed. Then you can concentrate on the smaller stuff.

Laurie and I worked with a client who was overwhelmed with clutter in almost every room in the house. We decided before beginning focused work on one room, we would first pull out any large unneeded items. After removing some bags of clothes and other items gathered for donation, large outgrown baby items and pet items, empty boxes, and other recyclables, the room already looked so much better. And all we had done was to declutter the big items! That initial decluttering burst was a great motivator for continued decluttering.

Start with Your Biggest Pain Point

Business people love talking about pain points, but it might not be a term with which you are familiar. Basically, a pain point is a problem that needs a solution. A pain point answers the question, "What's bothering you most?" If the kitchen is cluttered to the point that there's no empty surface on which to prepare food, that would definitely qualify as a pain point. Here are a few other descriptions of pain points:

- "My bed stays cluttered with books, toiletries, dirty clothes, etc."

- "I don't have a comfortable place to lie down to sleep unless I take some time to clear it."

- "I can't ever find anything! I waste a lot of time looking for things, and I buy things I know I already have because I can't find them."

- "Our dining room table is cluttered with paper, forcing us to eat in different areas of the house instead of having dinner together as a family."

- "I am sometimes late with bill payment, and I miss important events and deadlines because I can't seem to get a handle on the piles of paper."

- "My garage is so full of clutter I can't find what I need or even park my car in it."

- "I'm so embarrassed that every surface is covered with clutter. I haven't felt comfortable inviting guests over for a very long time."

I could go on and on, but you get the idea. Ask yourself (and others at your home) these questions to identify your pain points:

- What's bothering you most?

- What area or room do you totally avoid because you can't stand looking at the clutter?

- When people visit, which door always has to stay closed?

- What do other people in the home complain about most?

- What disrupts your daily home life most?

- Are any areas of the home so cluttered they can't be used as you intended?

Once you've identified your pain points, you might choose to start there.

Door and Commons

Another option for choosing where to begin with your decluttering is to focus on the door and the common areas. You'll be focusing on the most visible areas of your home, the areas that guests most commonly see. If your clutter has made you hesitant to invite guests into your home, this is a particularly appropriate strategy.

Put yourself in the role of a guest. Start at the front door. What is the state of your entryway? What is the first thing a guest would see? Which room would a guest walk into first, and what is the state of that room? Declutter each area in the order you come to it, and then move on to the next room. When you complete a decluttering session and come back for the next one, start at the front door again. If you've successfully maintained the areas you've already decluttered, you'll be able to move to a new area. If not, get the most visible areas decluttered (again) before moving on. Continue this process one area at a time in order of visibility. You'll be taking care of the common areas (most commonly visited areas of the home, including kitchen, guest bathroom, living room, etc.) before you address the more private areas (bedrooms, closets, drawers, basement, etc.). You can eventually declutter the entire house using this rule.

Just Start Somewhere!

Sometimes we can get so overwhelmed with the enormity of a project that we suffer from "the paralysis of overwhelm." This is especially true of perfectionists, who wait to get started because they want to make sure they have all of the available tools, have the full plan laid out, have consulted everyone involved, have all of the information they need, etc. Don't waste time overanalyzing. Just start somewhere!

When I talk to people about the need to declutter, they list so many excuses. I'll start decluttering "when I have more time, when the kids start back to school, over the holidays, over the summer, when I am recovering from my upcoming surgery, when I downsize, when I retire, when things settle down, when the kids leave for college," and on and on the excuses go.

Don't Wait Too Late

There is no perfect time to do this. Get started now. Even if you only get a little bit done, it's better than not starting at all! As a card-carrying perfectionist, I can still confidently attest that progress beats perfection every time. You can always go back and perfect things later, but if you wait too late to declutter, there is no going back. The longer you wait to deal with your accumulated possessions, the more difficult it will be.

Decluttering is hard work, both physically and mentally. Physically, it may require any or all of these actions: climbing stairs, picking up boxes and bins, pulling out multiple items, sorting through them, packing up and taking items for donation, recycling, or trash, and returning remaining items to their proper home. In addition, the mental work of making multiple decisions is difficult. If you wait too late to start decluttering, you may be incapable of either the physical or the mental work of decluttering, and you will place a huge burden on your family.

The people of Sweden are so much more prepared than those of us in the United States when it comes to decluttering. Margareta Magnusson describes a process called Swedish death cleaning in her book *The Gentle Art of Swedish Death Cleaning: How to Free Yourself and your Family from a Lifetime of Clutter*. Swedes take the tradition of death cleaning, which is usually completed sometime in their 50s or 60s, very seriously. As described by the author, Swedish death cleaning, (or *döstädning* in Swedish) "is a term that means that you remove unnecessary things and make your home nice and orderly when you think the time is coming closer for you to leave the planet."[23]

Although the name of the practice may sound morbid, Magnusson assures us this task is a pleasant one which reaps great rewards. From my own experience both personally and professionally, I heartily concur! When my husband and I recently downsized, we went through every single item we owned and made the decision of whether to keep it. Although the process was time-consuming, we found it quite enjoyable. We especially enjoyed completing the process together and including our adult children when possible. We love knowing that every single item we brought to our new space is something we use and love. We have gained so much peace of mind from knowing we won't be leaving our daughters with the enormous task of sorting through years of accumulated clutter. When my clients declutter, they report these same benefits.

Regarding loved ones left behind, Magnusson speaks candidly: "Do not ever imagine that anyone will wish—or be able—to schedule time off to take care of what you didn't bother to take care of yourself. No matter how much they love you, don't leave this burden to them."[24]

This may seem harsh, but if you have ever had to deal with someone else's things after their death, you understand completely. It's not fair to saddle our children and grandchildren with this responsibility. It's your stuff and consequently your responsibility.

Basic Decluttering Principles

Whatever area you've chosen or plan you're following, I hope you've made the decision to begin decluttering! Rather than give a step-by-step plan for decluttering individual areas, here are some basic decluttering principles you can use for any area.

Do I Love It? Do I Use It?

How do you go about making a decision about whether to keep an item? My favorite technique is to ask yourself two simple questions. Do I love it? Do I use it? If the answer to both of them is "Yes," it's an easy decision; that's an item you want to keep. If the answer to both is "No," that's also an easy decision; that's an item you don't need to keep. If you can only answer "Yes" to one of them, you need to think about it a little more deeply.

If you use something but don't love it, consider whether you have another item to accomplish the same purpose. If so, you may be able to give it up. How much room is it taking up? Also, consider how often you use the item. If it is used very infrequently, perhaps you could borrow one from someone else when it's needed again. How expensive would it be to replace it on the rare occasion when it is needed?

If you love something but never use it, why keep it? This is a common issue with sentimental items. We'll get into more details on dealing with sentimental keepsakes in the next chapter. For now, accept that it may be impossible to keep every single sentimental item you love. If you don't have the space, you'll have to make some tough decisions.

Pareto Principle

The Pareto Principle is attributed to a man named Vilfredo Federico Damaso Pareto, who was born in Italy in 1848. Pareto had noticed 20% of his garden's pea plants produced 80% of the healthy pea pods. He found this same proportion in the Italian economy, noting that 80% of the land in Italy was owned by 20% of the population. He coined a generalization from this imbalance that *80% of results will come from just 20% of the action.* This same principle can be observed in many business settings as well as in a host of personal examples.[25]

Professional organizers have observed this Pareto Principle to be generally true when it comes to our possessions. For any category of belongings, we tend to use 20% of them 80% of the time. Even when we have a large selection, we habitually choose our favorites. For example, if you own 100 shirts, you probably wear about 20 of them 80% of the time. If you own ten coffee mugs, you probably use two of them 80% of the time. Keeping this principle in mind can aid us in our decluttering efforts. Realizing we only use a relatively small percentage of the items in a category most of the time may give us the motivation we need to let go of more.

> ## We tend to use 20% of our belongings 80% of the time.

Save the Difficult for Last

I always advise clients to start with the easy stuff and save the more difficult stuff for last. Start with things you've known for a long time that you need to get rid of and save the most difficult stuff (like sentimental items) for last. This category is replete with memories and emotion. Marie Kondo's tidying process follows a very particular progression for good reason, and sentimental items are always handled last in Kondo's system.[26] By the time you get around to the sentimental items, you'll be more used to the process and hopefully you'll be more willing to let things go.

Container Concept

Credit for this term goes to Dana K. White. Although I had already used this principle many times, I didn't have a name for it until I heard it in one of Dana's podcast episodes.[27] You might assume the container concept is all about finding the right container. But the container concept goes much deeper than just a container.

A container's job is to contain. We usually think of the word contain in terms of holding something (as in, "that bin contains my collection of scrapbooking materials"). But contain also means "to hold or keep within limits; restrain" (as in, "I could hardly contain my curiosity") or "to halt the spread or development of; check" (as in, "Science sought an effective method of containing the disease").[28]

When we choose a home for a group of items (in the arranging step), we make a decision for not only where the items will live when they're not in use, but how many of them we can keep. In this situation, we're using the "keeps within limits" definition for the word container. If the items fit in the "container," they can stay. If the "container" is full and we want to add something, using the container concept means we have to remove something from the container before we can add the new item. In this context, a container can be a basket, a bin, a shelf, a room, or an entire house. It's simply a designated space that sets a limit.

Here's a practical example of how to utilize the container concept. Suppose you want to declutter your T-shirts because you know some are stained, ripped, or don't fit, and you've realized (because you understand the Pareto Principle) you wear only about 20% of them.

You open your dresser drawers only to discover that your T-shirt collection that was once contained in one drawer has miraculously expanded and now occupies two and a half drawers as well as the bedroom chair in a pile that is overflowing onto the floor. Sound familiar? After recovering from the shock, you're ready to take action so you follow these steps:

1. You decide one large dresser drawer of T-shirts should be plenty of T-shirts, so you choose one drawer as the container for your T-shirts.

2. You pull out every T-shirt from the drawers and put them on your bed, adding the pile from the chair and the floor.

3. You take a quick glance at the dirty clothes to see how many T-shirts are in there so you can take them into consideration as well.

4. You estimate how many T-shirts can fit into the drawer without the drawer being too crowded.

5. You look at each T-shirt individually and choose your favorite ones, limiting yourself to the number that will fit into the drawer.

6. Once the drawer is full, you get rid of the remaining shirts.

7. In the future, when you consider buying (or accepting a free) T-shirt, you keep in mind the container concept. You remind yourself that if you bring this shirt home, you'll have to get rid of one in the drawer (one in, one out).

8. You ask yourself if this shirt is truly worth bringing home.

The container concept is incredibly useful. You can utilize it for a broad range of applications. If you consider your kitchen cabinets as a container for dishes, you won't keep more dishes than will fit into the cabinets. If you consider your office desk and closet as a container for office supplies, you won't keep more supplies than will fit into them. On a broader scale, if you consider your house as a container for your belongings, you won't keep more than will fit into it, which means you won't rent a storage unit.

The container concept can even be used in a more theoretical sense. A 24-hour day is a container. If you fill it too full with optional events, you won't have enough space for your normal daily tasks, sleep, and time with family and friends.

One Area at a Time

If your clutter problem is extensive, even the prospect of decluttering may seem immense. Just like any large task, breaking it up into smaller pieces that can be accomplished in a small amount of time can keep you from feeling so overwhelmed. You can break a file cabinet down into one file folder or one drawer at a time, a closet into one category of clothing at a time, or a pantry into one shelf at a time. Taking small steps can still lead you to your goal without taking a significant amount of time away from your routine.

Try Aging Out Items

If you're really torn about whether to let some things go and you're stuck in a state of indecision, here's another strategy to give you a little more time to evaluate. Box up those items and label the box with a date. Labeling the box with a statement like "If not opened by 1/1/2022, donate all items" gives a specific target date. It also enables someone else who discovers the box to donate the items without hesitation. You can decide how long to give yourself. It could be a month, several months, or even a year. Make sure the box and the date are very visible. When the date arrives, donate anything you haven't used. Odds are you've even forgotten about the box. After all, you've proven during that period of time you didn't need those items, so letting them go should be easier now.

Daily Decluttering

This is my favorite decluttering tip of all! Even if you only incorporate this one habit, you'll see a big difference over time. I credit Lisa Woodruff of Organize365 for this tip.

Daily decluttering is a simple practice that takes very little time but yields far-reaching gains. All you need is one container somewhere on the main level of your house that is easy to access. Preferably this container would be one you don't need to keep, such as a shipping box or a large shopping bag. Whenever you see *anything* in your home you don't want to keep, immediately toss it into this container. When the container fills up, take it to your donation site of choice. Repeat this same process over and over.

The reason this practice is so powerful is it doesn't take much additional time, and it gets items out of your home quickly. It doesn't require you to stop what you're doing to spend a bunch of time decluttering. You simply work it into your daily routine. Even if you plan to do more extensive decluttering as well, get started with this habit now and continue it indefinitely!

Recruit Help if Needed

The bigger the team, the faster the work can be accomplished! If you live with others, get everyone in the home involved. If your extended family lives close enough and is willing to help, by all means take advantage of their offer! Younger generations tend to value experiences over things, and although they may not want many of your hand me downs, they may enjoy the experience of sorting through them with you. As you work together, tell them the stories behind the items. You'll accomplish important work while also making some great memories together. What a great combination! Close friends also make great helpers. If your friends need to declutter as well, consider helping each other or just encouraging each other and sharing your experiences.

You may also want to consider hiring a professional organizer. Their experience in helping clients declutter and their knowledge of the best solutions for organizing challenges could prove invaluable in helping you accomplish your goals. Some organizers also offer delivery of donations and recycling. You'll complete the decluttering work much faster than you would on your own.

I highly recommend hiring an organizer who is an active member of NAPO (National Association of Productivity and Organizing Professionals), the nationwide professional group for organizers. NAPO membership is a sign that an organizer is utilizing the experience of veteran organizers, continuing to learn, and keeping up with the trends in the industry. I am a member of NAPO and live in Kingsport, Tennessee. I provide custom one-on-one organizing services for homes and businesses in Northeast Tennessee and Southwest Virginia. If you live outside of that area, you can search on the NAPO website to find an organizer near you (www.napo.net). If there is no organizer living nearby, or if you prefer to do the work on your own with coaching from an organizer, I offer virtual organizing services as well.

ᘒ 13 ᘓ

What Are the Obstacles to Letting Go?

W hether you've started the decluttering process or not, just picking up this book and getting this far is evidence you're making progress. Remember, change happens in your mind before you ever take action! When you start decluttering, you are going to face some obstacles to letting go. I'd like to go ahead and prepare you for some of these obstacles so they don't surprise you and you'll be equipped to handle them. Forewarned is forearmed.

You will encounter many possessions, events on your calendar, or tasks on your To-Do list you know you should probably remove, but you may still struggle with the decision to let go. I know full well that the decluttering process is a difficult one, and I would never discount the complexity of emotions involved. However, working through these emotions is essential in order to find freedom from the hold our clutter has on us.

I will provide you with specific tips and motivation for each individual obstacle. Before discussing obstacles, let me remind you of a few of the Scriptures from previous chapters. When you find yourself hesitating to get rid of something, use the verses included in each section as your motivation to make difficult decisions.

Here are some common obstacles that could prevent you from letting go of physical clutter. Each section's title is a phrase I hear again and again.

Obstacles to Letting Go of Physical Clutter

"I Might Need It Someday!"

The underlying emotion inherent in this obstacle is fear. We are afraid if we give something away, we'll need it later and we won't have it. God promises if we put Him first, He'll make sure we have everything we need (Matthew 6:25-34, Psalms 55:22). Our Creator and Heavenly Father knows what we need, and He will provide for us. Do you trust Him with this promise?

This decluttering obstacle is probably the one I most commonly encounter. I am always amazed at the number of things people keep "just in case" they might need it someday. That consideration is extremely relative. We need to be able to determine the odds of us actually needing that item as well as the cost and difficulty of replacing it should we decide to let it go. In order to make a good decision about whether or not to keep an item, we need to evaluate two factors:

(a) the odds of us actually needing it again, and

(b) the cost and difficulty of replacing it should we decide to let it go.

I'll use two examples from decluttering my own home to illustrate how to make the decision of whether or not you might need something in the future. We had four bookshelves full of books, and we couldn't and didn't want to keep that many. Although we love to read, it is rare for us to reread a book. We've been transitioning to digital books anyway. If we did decide we wanted to read one of the books we got rid of, we could easily, with minimal expense, either borrow it from the library or buy another copy. The unlikely odds we would miss the books and the minimal cost of replacing them made thinning out our books much easier. For the books, both (a) and (b) are low, so the decision to let them go was easy.

On the other hand, when going through our tools, one item we kept "just in case" is our cordless drill. We don't use it very often, and we could probably borrow one if we did need it. But on the infrequent occasions when we do need it, it is very handy to have. It is a good quality tool that would be expensive to replace. For the cordless drill, although we don't need it very often, the probability of using it at some point (a) was high, and the replacement cost (b) was also high. These factors helped us decide it was best to keep the drill.

If we're doing a lot of decluttering (like most of us need to do), we're letting a lot of things go, likely in the hundreds and maybe even thousands. For the vast majority of those items, we never think of them again. We might remember one item or a few of them and regret having gotten rid of them. However, the space and freedom we've gained from getting rid of all of them outweighs the slight regret over a few items.

Joshua Fields Millburn and Ryan Nicodemus, The Minimalists, have turned this principle into their own personal rule of 20 Dollars, 20 Minutes. Their reasoning for this rule is that most of the time, anything they had let go of that they needed later could be replaced with $20 or less in 20 minutes or less. From the feedback they've gained from thousands of readers, their conjecture is that this holds true 99% of the time with 99% of the items and 99% of the people.[29] I for one think we should all test their theory.

Another commonly used method is any item you haven't used in a year or don't intend to use for a year is a good candidate for decluttering. This rule is another way to take into account the probability of using an item in the future. We may try to convince ourselves that since we rediscovered those art supplies we forgot we had, we'll definitely start painting again this weekend. But the best predictor of the near future is the near past. Odds are if you haven't used it in over a year, and especially if you didn't even remember you had it, you won't use it. Let it go. Does the rule work for every person, every item? Maybe not, but it's still a good rule to consider.

An important consideration is every item we keep "just in case" takes up valuable space in our home, space that could be put to far better use. Even more importantly, those "just in case" items that are boxed up and unused could be given to someone who needs them far more than you do. Are you a good steward of your God-given possessions if you keep them to yourself?

The following questions are helpful when considering what to do with an item you have been keeping "just in case":

- What is the situation for which I'm keeping this item "just in case"?

- How likely or unlikely is that situation?

- What is the worst that could happen if that situation happened and I didn't have the item?

- If I needed the item, how much time would it take to get another (either borrowing or buying)?

- How much would it cost?

- Do I trust God to take care of me?

Do you trust that God will take care of you if you put Him first? Are you willing to "live by faith and not by sight" (II Corinthians 5:7)? God LOVES to reward our faith! Remember Donna Waldron's story and the way God has taken care of her family when they put Him first? Put Him first, and let God take care of you and your family. Perhaps one day you'll have a remarkable story of faith to tell as well!

"I'm Keeping This for _____ !"

Have you saved things for your children, grandchildren, nieces, and nephews? You're in good company. Many homes have a large amount of space taken up by items held for someone else. *If* the person truly wants the items, and *if* you have plenty of room to store them, this is not a problem. However, more often than not, neither of these criteria has been met. The items are frequently saved assuming the person will want them in the future, but they've never actually been asked. The saved items are contributing a significant portion of the overall clutter of the home, and the space they occupy could be used for a much better purpose.

When you consider the space in your home that these saved items occupy and the time required to keep up with them, keep in mind that everything in our lives that doesn't align with our priorities takes our focus from what's most important. God urges us in Hebrews 12:1-2 to throw off anything that gets in the way of serving Him. He admonishes us in Matthew 25:14-30 to be good stewards of our time and our possessions.

The technique of saving items for someone else is often nothing more than a form of procrastination. The owner doesn't want to make the decision to discard the items or doesn't want to spend the time and effort required to sort through them and make decisions. The owner is simply keeping it because it's the easiest thing to do.

Taken to an extreme, your home can become a storage house for others. I have a client whose home is dangerously close to this level. Multiple closets are full of toys, school papers, and baby clothes that are all being saved for either her children (who are all grown now), future grandchildren, or nieces and nephews. It's much easier just to shut the closet door than it is to make decisions on all of the contents.

Try asking these questions to help you make a decision about saved items:

- Who am I saving this for?

- Do I know whether this person wants it? Can I find out now?

- If this person does want it, can I go ahead and give it? If not, when will I give it?

- If this person doesn't want it, am I willing to let it go? If not, why not? What's holding me back?

How do you overcome this obstacle? Before you keep those things any longer, ask the intended recipient if they want them, and be prepared to hear no. One way to accomplish this task quickly is to send a picture of the item with a text asking if they'd like to have it. Here's an example of a text you could send with a photo of the item: "I saw this while going through some items in my home and thought of you. Is this something you could use? No pressure! I can easily donate it if you don't need it." Give them "permission" to refuse it, and don't take it personally. Just because your family doesn't value the items you've saved for them doesn't mean they don't value you.

"It's Worth a Lot of Money!"

I encounter many people with a vast array of collectibles. A few common examples include Beanie Babies, Disney VHS tapes, Hummel figurines, sports trading cards, and Norman Rockwell plates. Often, they have collected them because they think at some point, they will be able to make a lot of money from them. But like the stock market, you almost never know the precise time to sell a collectible for a big profit. The reality is that the expected windfall almost never happens. Rarely does someone else think your collectible is worth as much as you do. Any item is worth only what you can get for it. It doesn't matter how much you think it's worth; it only matters what someone will pay you for it.

Remember the story of the rich fool in Luke 12 who had so many crops he had to build bigger barns to store them? It sounded like such a great idea, and he was looking forward to a life of ease. Jesus called the man a fool because he had put his trust in earthly treasures that would never last. God wants us to put our trust in Him alone. He wants to be our treasure.

Collectibles sit in containers on shelves for years for several reasons. You think the longer you hold onto it, the more it will be worth. You keep them a little longer, thinking they will be "worth something" soon. You don't know how to sell them. You don't take the time required to sell them. It takes time to research the price, take pictures, enter information, field inquiries, and pack for shipping. In the majority of cases, you won't get nearly as much money from selling these items as you are hoping. The process of selling is very time-consuming. Your time is probably your most precious commodity; don't underestimate its value. It's in your best interest to either go ahead and donate those items or to get someone who understands the process to sell them for you. Either way, that clutter category will be gone.

I am reminded of a client who had recently downsized and sought my help for unpacking. She had lived in her new home for a few months, and she had already unpacked all of the essentials. But there were still numerous boxes awaiting unpacking. Quite a few of the boxes contained various collectible figurines. She is probably expecting to get quite a bit of money from them. She didn't figure in the cost in terms of how much time it would take to sell them. She didn't consider where the collectibles would be stored in her smaller new home.

Think about the treasures you've saved and consider these questions:

- Are these items taking up space that could be better used?

- Do I have an accurate idea of how much they are worth now?

- When am I going to sell these?

- Do I want to take the time to sell them?

- Do I know how to do it? Or is there someone who can do it for me?

- Am I counting on the money from the sale of these items to give me financial security?

- Is my relationship with God my most valuable treasure?

- If I simply donated these items to a worthy cause, do I trust that God will take care of me?

Answering these questions may lead directly to your solution. If you realize that you're putting your faith in your treasures instead of God, this may spur you to action. If they're taking up a lot of space that you could use for something better, that fact may give you the motivation to let them go. If you've decided you don't have the expertise or don't want to take the time to sell them, you might want to ask for help. Spending a few minutes researching their value (especially if it's much lower than you anticipated) may lead you to consider simply donating them.

"I Paid Good Money for This!"

The hidden meaning behind this phrase is "I paid a lot of money for this, and I haven't used it as much as I thought. Now I feel terrible for getting rid of it because it seems like a waste of money." Talk about guilt!

Even if all of that is true, nothing you do now can change those facts. The money is already spent. Keeping the item out of a sense of guilt won't change the facts, and it definitely won't assuage the guilt. If anything, it will continue to reinforce it because every time you look at the item, you'll feel the guilt all over again. Once again, guilt alone isn't a good reason to save something.

A common example of this obstacle is buying materials for a craft you didn't end up doing or equipment for a sport in which you didn't participate like you thought. Some people might decide to keep these items in hopes that they will actually use them in the future. That sounds like good logic, but the odds are squarely against it.

> Guilt alone isn't a good reason to save something.

When my children were young, I went through a short phase of rollerblading. A good friend (a much younger friend) was into rollerblading, and she convinced me it would be fun. Have you seen many women in their late 30's rollerblading? Yeah, me neither. Maybe that should have been a clue. Anyway, I bought the expensive rollerblades, as well as knee pads, elbow pads, and gloves. I had a bike helmet I could use. I actually did enjoy rollerblading several times. I figured I would pick it up really quickly because I had been a regular at the Skate Inn during my junior high years.

It turns out stopping while rollerblading is a little trickier than I thought. After a monumental wipeout with painful scrapes, my rollerblading career was essentially over. I kept all of it for several more years thinking I would get back into it. But eventually I faced the facts and let them go. I hope the recipient of my donated rollerblading equipment had a longer and safer rollerblading career than I did.

What items are you holding onto because you paid good money for them? Here are some questions to consider:

- What hobbies (exercise, crafts, games, etc.) do I still have the supplies for but I haven't participated in them in a long time?

- Am I still physically capable of participating in the hobby?

- Am I still interested in the hobby? Or are there other hobbies I enjoy more now or new ones I am interested in trying?

- Do I find myself saying, "I should get back into _____ hobby," but I really don't have the desire to do so?

- If I had a free weekend ahead of me and could spend time getting those supplies back out and using them again, would I choose to do so?

- Am I keeping these hobby supplies only because I feel guilty about not using them?

Even if you haven't used the item you "paid good money for," just forgive yourself and move on. We've all made poor decisions with our money at one time or another. Let the item go, learn from your mistakes, and move on guilt-free.

We serve a God who is full of compassion. He doesn't want us to be burdened with guilt. Paul's letter to the

Philippians is a great example of forgiving yourself, resting in God's mercy, and moving on:

> Forgetting what is behind and straining toward what is ahead, I press on toward the goal to win the prize for which God has called me heavenward in Christ Jesus.
>
> Philippians 3: 13–14 (NIV)

"____ Gave It to Me!"

This category is not restricted to a gift you receive personally for a holiday or special occasion. It also includes items given by a friend or relative who thought you might need them or items you "inherited" (either literally or figuratively) from a loved one. These are all "gifts" in one way or another.

There are a number of reasons we might be reluctant to get rid of gifts. If the gift giver is someone very special to you and/or is deceased, that gift may hold more value to you. We may hold onto a gift not because we like it, but because we feel like it would be dishonoring the giver if we didn't keep it. In addition, we may fear if we give the gift away and the giver found out, it would hurt their feelings. Keep in mind that once something is given to you, it's yours. You can decide what to do with it. Giving it away doesn't mean you didn't appreciate the gift or the person who gave it. Guilt alone isn't a good enough reason to keep something.

No matter why you're hanging on to it, a gift that you no longer love and use is clutter. It's not doing you any good in your home; in fact, it's contributing to the general clutter that is having negative effects. Jesus is the ultimate giver! He was willing to give His very life for us.

Let's model Jesus by loving with actions and in truth (I John 3:16–18) and give so others can benefit.

My client Tasha had an aunt who was a crafter and showed hoarding behavior. That's a pretty dangerous combination because crafting requires a lot of stuff and it also generates a lot of stuff. She had several items her aunt had made for her, along with probably hundreds more she inherited when her aunt died. Her aunt had never done any decluttering, so naturally the house was full of stuff and required many people (including my client) to spend months going through everything. As we declutter together, we often find more items from her aunt. Initially my client was keeping everything her aunt had made. There was so much of it that it was taking up a lot of space. She finally decided that she couldn't keep all of them. She has a good strategy now for making choices about these items. If it's something she can use or display, she keeps it. If not, she lets it go guilt free.

Sometimes it can be helpful to turn a situation around to get a different perspective. Think about it this way: If you gave someone a gift and they didn't want it anymore, would you want them to keep it? Would you want them to feel burdened by it? I can easily answer this with an emphatic "NO!" I believe you would also want them to feel free to let it go without any guilt whatsoever. Chances are, the giver feels the same way.

- Have you kept gifts that you no longer love and use?

- What was your motivation to keep them?

- Is there a way you can use them or display them now?

- If not, could someone else benefit from them?

- What is holding you back from letting them go?

- Are you afraid the giver will be hurt if he/she finds out you don't have it anymore? If that happened, how would you handle it?

- If someone is holding onto a gift that you gave them only because they would feel guilty getting rid of it, would you feel okay about them letting it go?

When I have chosen to let a gift go that I no longer love or use, I thank God that I have everything I need and that I can trust Him to take care of me. I imagine what someone else might be able to do with it. I remember the positive benefits of letting go of clutter. I acknowledge to myself the thoughtfulness of the giver. If the giver found out I no longer had the item, I would say something like this: "It was kind of you to think of me. I really enjoyed your gift. I'm trying to do a better job of making sure everything I own is something I use and share anything I don't. Since I wasn't using it anymore, I decided to donate it to let someone else enjoy it like I did."

"It's Special!"

Sentimental items are probably the most difficult category to declutter. These objects bring back good memories of a loved one or a memorable experience (or both). There is nothing wrong with keeping some of them if they are still meaningful to you now and you still love and use them and you have room for them. So often, we have kept many mementos that we aren't using and haven't even looked at in many years.

The main reason people keep sentimental items is because of the memories they invoke. They fear that if they give the item away, they will lose the memory. But the memory isn't physically tied to the object; the memory is in our mind and in our heart. Even when you give away a memento, it doesn't mean you lose the memory associated with it.

How much space do sentimental items take up in your home? Unless you have a huge home, it's just not possible or practical to keep everything! I frequently tell clients overrun with mementos, "If everything is special, nothing is special." It reminds me of reading a book and highlighting every word. Nothing would stand out because it would all be highlighted. If we have an inordinate number of mementos, we probably have very low criteria for what we define as special.

> # If everything is special, nothing is special.

Those boxes of mementos stored in the attic for 50 years may have been saved because they were special at one time. But how special is something if it's been boxed up for 50 years and never viewed? Your home is not intended to be a museum. Your sentimental items are taking up space that could be used for much better purposes. If an item still "brings you joy," in the words of Marie Kondo, use it or display it!

Take the time to sort through those boxes, preferably with a family member or friend. Take those mementos out, relive the memories, tell the stories about them, and then do something with them besides just stuffing them all back into the box indefinitely! You can find a wealth of ideas on Pinterest for turning your mementos into something useful or visually appealing.

I love this excerpt from a blog post by Darla DeMorrow, author of *SORT and Succeed*, on emotional strategies for decluttering: "Visualize decay. I've seen so many things molded and rotted, and of no use to anyone. Think of decades-old baby items in the basement or attic. Instead of falling apart and being no use to anyone, those clothes, toys, and baby care items could be useful to someone else less fortunate than you."[30]

Here is an example from my own home. I knew we wouldn't have room in our small loft for my wedding dress. Like most eighties' brides, I carefully preserved my dress in a box and saved "just in case." I asked my adult daughters whether they would like to save the dress or a portion of it for a future wedding. One daughter was interested, so we looked at some repurposing ideas on Pinterest. I saved a few pieces to make a bouquet wrap and a hair comb for her wedding day. I had a small decorative pillow made from a few other pieces. This "downsized" the box but also allowed me to save some parts of the dress.

Before you get all excited and hop on Pinterest, let me warn you. The danger of this idea is that you'll keep a whole lot of mementos so "someday" you can get on Pinterest and turn them into something useful or beautiful. And you just might. But then again, you also just might stick them back where you found them and never touch them again while they continue to clutter your home and never get used or displayed.

Unless those sentimental items are extremely important to you, consider letting at least some of them go. Recall the discussion of stewardship from Chapter 7. When we have a large accumulation of belongings stuffed inside boxes and bins for years without being touched, how can we consider ourselves good stewards?

Are sentimental items part of your clutter problem?

- What kind of sentimental items are you holding on to?

- Do you have sets of china, jewelry, quilts, old clothing, greeting cards, or old toys?

- Have you saved your children's special T-shirts for years intending to have a T-shirt quilt made?

- Are you afraid that if you let mementos go, you'll forget the person or event they remind you of?

How can you successfully navigate this obstacle? Be honest about whether or not these mementos are truly still meaningful to you. If they are, figure out a way to use them. If they aren't, let them go.

Be realistic about your odds of actually completing the projects you intend with the mementos. Give yourself a deadline to complete it, and if you don't meet the deadline, either hire someone to complete the project (if you can afford it), or just let the items go.

If you are afraid you'll forget, consider other ways to ensure the memory won't be lost. Could you take a picture of the mementos, write about them, tell a family member about them, or record a story about them?

"I Don't Have Time"

Next to the "But it's special!" obstacle, this one is either first or a close second. I feel the pressure as well. There are so many demands on our time. Very few of us have unlimited free time to accomplish projects, no matter how much we want to work on them. Lack of time can hinder us from accomplishing decluttering and organizing projects with our possessions. It can also prevent us from confronting schedule and attention clutter.

> Too often we use our schedule to define who we are, instead of letting who we are define our schedule.

This is a widespread problem, especially in a culture where being busy is largely viewed as a virtue. We talk about being busy like it's a badge of honor, a measure of our importance. Too often we use our schedule to define who we are, instead of letting who we are define our schedule. Our schedule needs to reflect our values and priorities.

As always, God's Word provides inspiration for using our time wisely and for remembering our time on Earth is brief.

> Be very careful, then, how you live—not as unwise but as wise, making the most of every opportunity, because the days are evil."
>
> Ephesians 5:15–16 (NIV)

> Show me, Lord, my life's end and the number of my days; let me know how fleeting my life is.
>
> Psalms 39:4 (NIV)

We've already established that wasted time is a consequence of clutter. Addressing our clutter will give us more time. Yet we have trouble finding the time to declutter. It sounds like a catch-22 scenario. If we make time to declutter, we'll gain back so much more time than we lost. I've seen this happen with clients over and over again. It really does work, and it's worth it!

It's a simple matter of a return on our investment. We understand this principle as it applies to our finances. If we invest some money into home improvements by updating our kitchen, we may get a good return in terms of a faster sale and possibly a better offer. When we invest some time into decluttering and organizing, we gain back even more time.

My client Lois invested a few hours into professional organizing services for her master bedroom and bathroom. She reports that ever since then, getting ready for work every morning has been much quicker and more peaceful. My client Liza invested in a few hours of professional organizing services for her kitchen. Because she can now easily find what she needs, meal preparation and cleanup is faster and less stressful.

One specific practice that frees up considerable time is working on daily routines like dishes, laundry, and daily pickup (Chapter 12, p. 118-121). By perfecting and maintaining daily routines, you will greatly increase your available time. A technique that is effective for decluttering but takes almost no time is Daily Decluttering (Chapter 12, p. 132). It's easy and effective. Small task, big gains.

Keep in mind that there is no perfect time to declutter. The sooner you start, the sooner progress is made and the momentum will carry you forward. Progress beats perfection every time! Waiting too late can lead to dire consequences. We don't want to wait until we're physically or mentally incapable of doing the hard work. And we don't want to leave a burden for our loved ones. (Chapter 12, p. 124–126).

It's easy to get overwhelmed thinking about the amount of time you'll need to complete these tasks. But if we envision it one room at a time, or one drawer at a time, one closet at a time, etc., it's not so overwhelming. Just like any large task, decluttering can be broken up into lots of smaller ones. You could literally spend five minutes a day on this and you'd accomplish a lot.

If the idea of decluttering is still more than you can bear, you may need to consider the possibility of recruiting help (Chapter 12, p. 133). You may be in a stage of life in which you are just struggling to survive day to day. If you have multiple small children, have an extremely demanding job with late hours or are holding down multiple jobs, have health issues yourself, or are caring for aging parents, you literally may not have the time and/or energy to devote to decluttering. If this applies to you, it's probably time to call in reinforcements. You may be fortunate enough to have family members or friends who are willing to help you. A professional organizer can greatly accelerate the decluttering process by working alongside you to help you reach your goals or by giving you a step by step plan specific for your situation.

⬥ 14 ⬥

How Do I Prevent Future Clutter?

N o matter what kind of change we're working on in our lives, isn't preventing backsliding always the biggest challenge? Even if we've successfully conquered a huge challenge, our celebration can be dampened by fear of relapse. Maybe you've been in this position before with other habit changes. You worked hard and successfully changed a long-standing habit. You were determined not to go back to the way it was before. You may have even had the best of intentions and a battle plan. But eventually you went back to your old ways. I understand. I've been there, too, with many habit changes. It's incredibly frustrating.

How do we prevent returning to old habits? How do we know it's going to "stick" this time? How can we be assured that this time, it's really going to last? If we start backsliding, how can we recover quickly so it won't get completely out of control? Here are a few tools and some encouragement for your decluttering journey.

Continue to Declutter

Decluttering isn't a one-time event. It's a way of life. We have to continue shedding our unnecessary belongings, tasks, and distractions in order to achieve long-term success.

Prioritize the Daily Routines

Vigilance in those daily routines of dishes, laundry, and daily pickup (Chapter 12, p. 118–121) will do wonders for preventing re-accumulation of clutter. There will doubtless be times in your life when schedules are infinitely hectic, and you may get briefly off track. For instance, it's common to get a little behind on routine tasks during the holidays, the week of a big move, or after an unexpected crisis. But these situations should be the exception, not the rule. Maintaining daily routines is critical for staying organized. Consistency with daily routines is a prerequisite to maintaining order. I've never witnessed a single home achieve order without consistent daily routines.

- Have you established daily routines for dishes, laundry, and daily pickup?

- How consistent have you been with each routine?

- What is working or not working with each routine?

- Have you spoken with others in the home about how the routines are going and how they could be adjusted?

Daily routines are also helpful for preventing re-accumulation of schedule clutter. Each time you reach for your calendar to potentially add an activity, establish a routine of pausing to consider these questions:

- Does this activity align with my priorities?

- If I add this activity, will I still have adequate time for Bible study, prayer, and gathering with other believers?

- If I add this activity, will I have enough time for myself and for my family?

Prioritizing daily routines can also help us monitor attention clutter. Monitoring and limiting daily smartphone use is essential for preventing attention clutter. A regular habit of time in God's Word and prayer, especially in the morning, can center our attention for the day. We can choose to feed our minds with wholesome books, music, podcasts, etc. that will help us focus our thoughts on godly principles.

Daily Decluttering

I can't overemphasize the effectiveness of daily decluttering. Do you have your daily decluttering container as described in Chapter 12, p. 132? Have you started tossing items into it the moment you realize you don't need them? If not, stop reading and get it set up. I'll be waiting for you right here. If you've already got that practice going, pat yourself on the back and read on.

Move (or Just Pretend)

Nothing forces you to face the reality of how much you own like packing for a move. About three years ago, my husband Eric and I downsized in a big way into a space less than one third the size of our home. A few months later, we moved into an even smaller space. We felt such freedom as we let go of everything we didn't love and use.

I'm partially joking about scheduling a move. It's a bit extreme and impractical to move just to declutter. But you can always pretend you're moving. A high school friend told me about her family's annual tradition. Once a year, they pretend they are moving. They go around the whole house looking at all of their stuff and ask themselves, "If we were moving, would this item survive the move?" If not, they donate it or sell it at a garage sale. What a terrific idea!

Simplify Whenever Possible

Continually look for the simplest way to accomplish a task. Look for the route that requires the least amount of supplies and time. Ask yourself, "Is this really necessary? Could this be done in a simpler way that takes less time? Could I use something I already have instead of buying new supplies?"

If you're a perfectionist like me, it isn't always easy to simplify a process. Perfectionists like using the best possible tools to accomplish a task. Making do with something less than optimal is difficult. Perfectionists tend to latch onto a task and get deeply entrenched in it without pausing to consider whether it's a good use of time.

That unique specialty kitchen gadget you just have to buy (I'm looking at you, strawberry stem remover, pickle picker, and butter spreader for an ear of corn) takes up space that could be used by a more versatile tool like a knife and a fork. During our downsize, I gave away my bread machine. I loved it, and I used it occasionally, but it's a fairly large appliance that only accomplishes one purpose. I can (and do, sometimes) make bread without a bread machine. Or I can (and do, often) just buy a loaf of bread. Understand I am saying this even though I LOVE kitchen tools.

I learned a great example of simplifying from my client Patty. She had gotten frustrated with how many gift-wrapping supplies she had and how much space they occupied. She no longer wanted to store multiple rolls of paper, multiple sizes and styles of gift bags, tissue paper, bows, ribbons, tape, tags, and embellishments. She opted to choose one neutral color of wrapping paper and gift bag and one color of bows and ribbons (a champagne color paper and gift bag with black ribbons and bows). It would be appropriate for gifts for any occasion, and it would simplify gift wrapping.

Prevent Inflow

I've discussed plenty of techniques for dispensing with unneeded belongings. But I haven't yet addressed ways to prevent the inflow of new stuff. Over-acquiring is a BIG problem. You can declutter until the cows come home, but if you keep bringing more stuff in at a rapid clip, you'll never solve your clutter problem.

Respectfully Decline "Gifts"

I have already addressed the subject of gifts as a decluttering obstacle. But in that section of the book, I was talking about gifts you have already brought into your home. What if you refuse to accept a "gift" in the first place? In the case of items passed on from a deceased loved one, there often isn't any other choice in the midst of the crisis but to just transfer everything from one place to another and deal appropriately with them at a later time.

But in many situations, you have a choice. When someone offers you something, it is entirely your choice whether or not to accept it. I'm not talking about being rude here. If someone hands me a wrapped gift on a special occasion, I will always take it and thank them. What I'm referring to is when someone is offering to give you something because they think you might be able to use it. This person may have finished using it themselves, or they may have seen a good deal at the store and thought of you. Or they may have picked it up from the side of the road and decided you needed it (true client story).

Let's say you decide quickly you don't need an item someone is offering to give you. If you accept it, it will add to your clutter. But you certainly don't want to hurt their feelings. After all, it was nice of them to think of you.

First, always thank them for their thoughtfulness. Then make a quick decision. You can just accept it and then donate it. But here's the rub—you have not only added to your clutter, you've added an errand to your schedule. Granted, if you have a daily decluttering container and the item is small, it's not a big deal. But what if the item is large or if there are multiple items? What if the donation destination is out of your way, or there are multiple stops required? If you donate it and they ask about it later, what will you say? It just got really complicated, and your goal is to simplify, not complicate.

It is perfectly acceptable to say, "No, thank you." You can still communicate it in a nice way. When working with clients, I give them permission to blame me. Here are a few sample fictional conversations to consider:

Response 1: "How nice of you to think of me and to deliver it! I really appreciate your thoughtfulness. Actually, I don't think I can use that right now, but I'm pretty sure _____ (a person/charity you are familiar with) could use it."

Response 2: "How kind of you! I have been decluttering, and I'm limiting what I bring into my house. I'm sorry, but I'll have to pass. But I really appreciate you thinking of me!"

One In, One Out

This is an extremely simple but effective strategy to prevent accumulation. It works perfectly when you have used the container concept to determine the right amount that is just enough but not too much to fill the space and meet your needs. Let's say your shoe organizer has enough space for 30 pairs of shoes and you are satisfied with the ones you have. You're out shopping and you fall in love with a pair of shoes. You try them on, and they fit perfectly!

Before you purchase the shoes, consider whether this pair is better than one of the pairs you own. If not, walk away (wearing your old shoes). If they are, buy the shoes, but be sure to get rid of a pair when you get home. You'll still have the right number of shoes to fit into your shoe organizer. If you're still in the decluttering process, try using a one in, two out strategy. Better yet, try a one in, three out (or more) to speed up your decluttering efforts.

We've already touched on using this same strategy with your schedule (Chapter 10, p. 95). Before adding an event to your schedule, make every effort to remove another. This simple strategy is very effective for preventing re-accumulation of any type of clutter.

Remember, decluttering is a continuous process, not a one-shot deal.

Don't Add Items to Your Shopping Cart

When we shop and we see something we like, it's easy to just mindlessly toss it into our shopping cart. Then when we get to the cash register, we buy it without thinking twice. One of my clients shared a new strategy she had implemented that had successfully decreased her buying. When she sees an item she wants that isn't on her list, instead of immediately placing the item into her shopping cart, she keeps walking. If she forgets about the item by the end of the shopping time at that store, she figures she didn't need the item that much and has no regrets. If she continues to think about the item during the rest of the shopping time and decides she really needs it, she goes back to get it.

Scrutinize Potential Purchases

This is a similar strategy to the previous one but requires more thought. When you see an item you are considering buying, take some time to really evaluate it. This list of questions can help you decide:

- Do I have a use for it right now or in the near future, or is it another "just in case" item?

- Am I buying this because it's a good deal, not because I need it?

- Do I know exactly where I would put this? Is there room for it?

- Is this usable now as is?

- Does it have to be repaired or altered?

- Do I have to wait until sometime in the future to use it?

- If this is a purchase for someone else, am I absolutely sure the person would love it and use it?

When scrutinizing a clothing purchase for instance, the question of whether the item is usable now is especially important. Purchasing an item of clothing that won't fit until you lose some weight will give you a negative visual reminder every time you look at it. If it needs to be altered, you have to consider the additional time required to fix it or deliver it to someone who can.

Here are a few more potential purchases that qualify for extra scrutiny: a picture that would be perfect for my bedroom, only with a black frame instead of the current brown one; the baseball glove that would probably be perfect for my son in a few years; bottles of scented soap at a discounted price that would make a good gift for someone someday, etc.

When you're shopping and see something that seems perfect for a friend or family member, resist buying it for them. Try texting them a picture of it and telling them you thought they might like. If they don't reply and ask you to get it, move on. If it's a local store, you can always come back later. Better yet, they can purchase it. You are decluttering. Be mindful that others are doing the same. You don't want to add to your own clutter or anyone else's.

Considering the following questions will encourage more mindful shopping. If we all took the time to deliberate on potential purchases, we would cut down on our spending considerably and wind up with much less clutter:

1. Can I afford this now? Will buying it hurt me financially? For example, will I have to put it on a credit card, adding to my debt?

2. Will this item benefit my life? What specific value will it bring?

3. Is there a better use for this amount of money?

4. Can I wait a while before making a decision? Maybe thinking about it will change my perspective.

5. What other actions does this purchase require of me? For example, what will it require as far as upkeep?

6. Am I purchasing this to replace something in my home? Do I know what I will do with the old one? Will it become clutter, or am I willing to let it go?

7. Will purchasing this item require me to purchase another item(s) in addition to this one?

8. Will purchasing this item require me to commit to a particular activity?

In terms of what an item costs besides money, we rarely delineate all of the tasks or estimate the amount of time these tasks will require. Nor do we figure in the cost of additional purchases that will result. Witness these examples: That cute dress you just bought looks perfect on you. But you don't have shoes that match, so you'll need to factor that in. It would also look better with a belt and some jewelry that match, and you don't have either of those. Purchasing scrapbooking materials because you've always wanted to make a scrapbook for each of your seven children sounds noble, but are you sure you have the time to accomplish this monumental task?

That's a lot of factors to consider, right? Mindful, intentional shopping takes some serious reflection and discipline. Although purchasing an item is an exceedingly easy process, the ramifications can go deeper than we care to admit. Choose carefully. Choose mindfully. Choose less to gain more.

Shop with Intention

Since the majority of our inflow comes from shopping, it only makes sense that reducing our shopping time would be a helpful behavior change. When we plan our shopping in advance with a list and a clear idea of what we need, we're less likely to overbuy. While I love this mindset of intentionality, I also acknowledge that for many people, shopping is an enjoyable pastime and social activity. Is it possible to shop casually without overbuying and contributing to clutter? It's possible, but it's certainly not easy. Using the other tips for preventing inflow will improve your odds of success.

If shopping with a friend is a favorite activity primarily because of the companionship, why not consider going for a walk in a park together instead? You'll enjoy the companionship but will also benefit your health. There are many alternative plans that include social interaction but won't result in impulse purchases. Use your imagination; the sky's the limit! This tip (as well as the next two) was inspired by a mindful shopping blog post.[31]

Take a Break from Shopping

Decide on a set time period during which you will only purchase needed groceries and consumables like regularly used toiletries, paper products, etc. During that time, limit yourself to buying only what is absolutely necessary. You'll have to say "no" to that ab roller, fake succulent, and lobster claw oven mitts during the break. You may have to wrap a reminder note around your billfold and/or credit cards. If you're an online shopper (who isn't these days?), perhaps you'll need a note on all of your digital devices. You could either use something physical like a sticky note or use an image as a screensaver that will remind you of your shopping break. Tell your spouse and close friends about your moratorium. Maybe you could use an accountability partner who could join you in the challenge.

Even if that time period is small, it will be eye-opening. Sometimes we don't even realize how much we buy on impulse.

Consider the Cost in Terms of Hours Worked

Figure out a rough estimate of your hourly wage. If you're not working outside of the home right now, use your spouse's gross income for this calculation. Or estimate what it would cost to have someone come in and do the work you do. Look at the price of the item you want to buy, and figure out how many hours you or your spouse would have to work to buy it.

As an example, let's say you earn $25 per hour after taxes. You're considering purchasing a new outfit costing a total of $200. Is the outfit worth eight hours of your work time? Considering the cost of the item in this way may help you gain some much-needed perspective.

Put it on a Wishlist

Adding an item you want to buy to a wish list instead of buying it immediately is another technique to help you pause to consider a purchase. This practice ensures the item isn't forgotten. If a birthday or holiday is approaching, the wish list will generate gift ideas for others. A few suggestions for a wish list include paper, the Notes app on your phone, Amazon, or AnyList (a free app for storing any kind of list).

Putting items on a wish list is useful as a parenting strategy. When my children were younger, if they saw something they wanted but didn't need right then (or at all), I would add it to a wish list. Then I always had ideas at the ready for birthdays, holidays, or special rewards. It helped reduce nagging. If they never mentioned it again, that was an indication it wasn't a priority. It was a way of giving both of us time to think about it while also ensuring it wasn't forgotten.

Change Your Daily Habits

I've discussed many different strategies, tools, and tricks you may find helpful in your efforts to stay clutter-free and to maintain order in your home. While these strategies can be helpful, the main factor in determining your success comes down to consistent daily habits. Once you have cleared your clutter and established homes for everything remaining, you have to get into the habit of putting items back where they belong after you use them. It needs to be a dependable routine for everyone at your home. While it's unreasonable to expect a routine to be followed 100% of the time, exceptions should be infrequent. If you are consistent with routines the majority of the time, occasional lapses won't set you back too far and you'll be able to get back on track quickly.

Resist the urge to temporarily toss items on the floor, the couch, the kitchen counter, or other surfaces just because it's easier than putting them away. The floor, the couch, the kitchen counter, and the tops of furniture pieces aren't good choices for item homes. When you return from a trip, if at all possible, go ahead and unpack completely and get back into your routines. When a load of laundry comes out of the dryer, fold and put it away so you don't end up with piles or baskets of clothes everywhere. After a shopping trip, put away your purchases. Get children into the habit of putting dirty clothes, school work, toys, etc. where they belong on a daily basis.

You might have rolled your eyes while reading the last paragraph because of course you already know you should stick to routines like these. But just because something is simple doesn't mean it's easy or that most people do it. If you haven't established routines like these before, don't expect the change to be automatic or simple. You will be tempted to revert to old ways. That's a natural temptation for any habit change. Changing our habits can be a challenge, but it's doable. And it's certainly worth it.

Internalize the Habit Changes

Changes in behavior have several layers. The outer layer and the one we tend to think about most is a change of outcome, like losing weight (*what we get*). The second layer is changing our process, which involves changes of habit and systems (*what we do*). We already know unless we change our habits consistently, we won't get the desired outcomes. But the deepest layer of change involves changing our identity, or what we believe about the world and about ourselves (*who we are*). Long-lasting change is most effective when it reaches into this layer.

James Clear's bestselling book *Atomic Habits*[32] illustrates this difference by comparing two people who want to quit smoking. Both are offered a cigarette. The first one says, "No, thanks. I'm trying to quit." The second says, "No, thanks. I'm not a smoker." While the difference in terms of the words isn't much, there is a fundamental difference in how these two people see themselves. The first person still identifies as a smoker, albeit one trying to quit. The second person has made this behavior change a part of their identity. They no longer consider themselves a smoker. It's a subtle change in terms of the words but a huge change in the mindset.

> The deepest layer of change involves changing our identity.

When you decide the kind of person you want to be and identify yourself that way, ask yourself what that kind of person would do, and do it! Model your behavior according to that identity. Ask yourself questions like, "What would a clutter-free person do? What would a person who views their possessions as a gift from God do? What would a person who wants to use their time to serve God do? What would an organized person do?" When you've answered those questions with actions, work on consistently performing those actions. Focus on being that kind of person. Prove to yourself that you *are* that person. And watch the way you word it in your thoughts and your speech, because it really does make a difference. It's great to say or think, "I'm going to get organized," or "I want to get rid of my clutter." But it's an entirely different mindset to say, "I am a person who makes good choices with my time and my belongings," or "I am a person who values order."

Learn What Motivates You

The more we know ourselves, the better we'll be at choosing approaches that work for us. A co-worker raves about their success in getting fit using new group exercise classes at their gym. Another credits their success to a free app for logging their workouts and food choices. While both of those programs might have impressive success rates, they may not be the best choice for you. Understanding how we respond to expectations, both ones we place on ourselves (like making a New Year's resolution) and those imposed by others (like meeting a work deadline), can help us choose methods that will work for changing our habits.

In her book *The Four Tendencies*[33], Gretchen Rubin divides people into four categories by the way they respond to expectations.

- *Upholders* readily meet both outer expectations and inner expectations. Sounds perfect, right? As an upholder, I can tell you one of the downsides is that it's easy to latch onto a task that isn't the best use of time and have difficulty letting it go.

- *Questioners* will respond to an expectation only if it makes sense to them. They question all outer expectations and will meet them only if they believe they are justified. In reality, they respond only to inner expectations.

- *Obligers* have a difficult time meeting inner expectations, but they do well with meeting outer expectations. They are much more successful if someone else is counting on them to meet the expectation.

- *Rebels* resist all expectations, outer and inner. They will respond to an expectation if it's their idea on their time frame and if they feel like it. When someone imposes an outer expectation on them, they are usually driven further away from the desired behavior.

Obligers are the most common of the four tendencies and also the group that benefits most from using their tendency in their favor. Obligers meet outer expectations but have a hard time meeting inner expectations. If they have a goal for themselves (inner expectation) but don't have some sort of accountability (outer expectation) tied to it, they aren't likely to succeed. The critical missing element for obligers is accountability. There are plenty of ways for obligers to include accountability to improve their odds of success. Methods can be as simple as just telling someone about their goal or as complex as setting up a system that will automatically trigger an unpleasant consequence (such as an embarrassing social media post) if the obliger doesn't wake up in time to stop it.

Upholders will probably be the group that is most likely to keep clutter from reaccumulating. Once an upholder has set up a routine for daily habits that works for them, they are liable to continue them and to hold others in the household accountable for maintaining the habits as well. Upholders need to make sure that the routines they establish are reasonable to maintain. They also need to give grace to themselves and others when the routines slip temporarily during periods of high demand, knowing that they will be able to get back on track soon.

Questioners need to focus on making sure the daily habits they establish are necessary, effective, and fit well into other household practices. They may feel the need to continually tweak their routines until they make sense to them and meet their standards. Although this process of revision may seem unnecessary to other household members, it is an important part of internalizing the habits for Questioners.

Maintaining habits and preventing clutter from reaccumulating will likely be most difficult for *Rebels*. They may in fact rebel at the very idea of routines, much less daily ones. Above all of the other tendencies, they need to be given the opportunity to come up with the ideas themselves and the freedom to do things their own way. Other household members may find their reluctance to conform to established routines incredibly frustrating. But the more a Rebel is pushed to do something they don't want to do, the less likely they are to do it. As frustrating as this sounds to someone who's not a Rebel, keep in mind that a Rebel just may be the one whose seemingly outlandish ideas and sporadic behaviors produce the most favorable outcomes.

Using the ideas from *The Four Tendencies* has benefited my own practices and allowed me to better understand my clients. Although just figuring out which tendency you fit into is interesting, the real magic comes in using this information to tailor your approach to behavior change. It's a simple concept to understand, but the applications are phenomenally beneficial.

Be Kind to Yourself

In spite of our best efforts, none of us will incorporate habit changes perfectly. Even with a stellar plan, motivation galore, and a steady diet of God's Word, we will inevitably stumble at some point. Setbacks are part of the process of learning. After all, we are human! When we stumble, we need to extend the same grace to ourselves as God extends to us. Guilt and shame will only drag us down.

Consider the way loving parents teach their children a new skill, like learning to ride a bicycle without training wheels. They patiently explain it, model it, and encourage them to practice. When the children are practicing and they stumble, the parents aren't surprised. They know that stumbling is part of the learning process. They continue to encourage them with phrases like: "That's ok; keep trying!", "You're getting the hang of it!", and "Don't worry. It will get easier." They are gentle and positive.

Be gentle with yourself when you struggle with habit changes. Silence those negative tapes that play in your head. Setbacks are a completely normal part of the process! It does no good to continue to beat ourselves up about a mistake. In fact, it is counterproductive to our efforts. Hop right back on the wagon and move on. Continue to employ those daily habits that will enable you to become the person you wish to be.

�֍ 15 ☙

What Does the Bible Say About Changing Habits?

Even though I am sitting alone in my quiet office, I have felt all along that we were taking a journey together. Yes, I realize that sounds kind of mushy and sentimental. But I want you to know I have prayed so much that my words would somehow challenge and inspire each of you. I have prayed from the very first step of writing that God would give me the words that would be most helpful. Any skills I have for organizing or writing have come straight from God, and I want my words to glorify Him above all.

Sometimes just the right creative ideas and helpful resources shared at the right time can give us exactly what we need to change our habits. However, God's Word and His Spirit inside of us are the most powerful tools of all. These passages from the Bible can provide the inspiration and the words of encouragement you need to be successful.

God's Spirit in Us

As Christians, God has given us His Spirit, a part of His very essence to live inside us. The Creator of the Universe, the all-knowing, all-powerful God has deemed us worthy of housing a part of Himself inside of us. It's definitely not because we are inherently worthy, but because of Jesus' sacrifice on our behalf. I don't know about you, but for me, this is nothing short of mind-boggling.

> God's Word and His Spirit inside of us are the most powerful tools of all.

> If you love me, keep my commands. And I will ask the Father, and he will give you another advocate to help you and be with you forever—the Spirit of truth. The world cannot accept him, because it neither sees him nor knows him. But you know him, for he lives with you and will be in you.
>
> John 14:15–17 (NIV)

We can find reassurance deep in our hearts that God is with us (literally) in this journey. He knows every challenge we have, every goal we've set, every yearning in our heart. He's forever on our team. He wants us to succeed. God's Spirit isn't just some theoretical reassuring feeling or wisp of a ghostlike wind. God's Spirit is real, and it is powerful.

The Power of God's Spirit

The same Spirit that had the power to raise Jesus from the dead is living inside of us. Unbelievable! God's Spirit has the power to do anything in our life that is in line with God's Word and His purpose. Decluttering our stuff, our schedule, and our mind is in line with God's Word and His purpose. Knowing we have the power of the Holy Spirit working within us should give us a huge boost of confidence!

> And if the Spirit of him who raised Jesus from the dead is living in you, he who raised Christ from the dead will also give life to your mortal bodies because of his Spirit who lives in you.
>
> Romans 8:9–11 (NIV)

Changing our habits is hard work. I'm so glad I don't have to rely on my own strength and willpower! Particularly in areas where we need to say "No" (not taking on too much in our schedule, not buying that unnecessary thing), we don't have to do this on our own. We don't have to grit our teeth and say "No." We have God's grace helping us say "No."

> For the grace of God has appeared that offers salvation to all people. It teaches us to say "No" to ungodliness and worldly passions, and to live self-controlled, upright and godly lives.
>
> Titus 2:11-12 (NIV)

Crucified with Christ

When we made the decision to trust God and to make Him ruler of our lives, our old self was crucified with

Christ. We were raised to a new life just as Christ was raised from the dead.

> I have been crucified with Christ and I no longer live, but Christ lives in me. The life I now live in the body, I live by faith in the Son of God, who loved me and gave himself for me.
>
> Galatians 2:20 (NLT)

Our decision to serve God wasn't just a one-time thing. Our old self with its habits and its sins will always try to creep back into our lives. Once we start making the changes outlined in this book, we shouldn't be surprised when we find ourselves falling back into old habits. In a sense, every one of us has to decide each day whether we will serve God or serve our own interests. Will we let God take His rightful place on the throne of our lives? Or will we climb back up there and make decisions serving our own best interests with no thought to eternity? It all comes down to trusting that God always has our best interests at heart and that He always knows best.

Completing a Good Work

We must be patient with ourselves. We are a beautiful work in progress. Whatever stage we're in, recognize we are moving towards our Father, and He is waiting with open arms. He always has been, and He always will be.

Paul and Timothy wrote Philippians as a letter to the Christians in Philippi. Having spent time in ministry with the Philippians, they knew intimately the church's strengths and weaknesses. While the Christians had made progress during Paul and Timothy's time there, there was still much work to do. Paul expresses confidence that God will continue to work in their lives to complete the work that had been started.

> I thank my God every time I remember you. In all my prayers for all of you, I always pray with joy because of your partnership in the gospel from the first day until now, being confident of this, that he who began a good work in you will carry it on to completion until the day of Christ Jesus.
>
> Philippians 1:3–6 (NIV)

Just like the Philippians, we are not there yet, but we're on our way. Anytime we strive to align ourselves more closely to God's Word and the image of Jesus, God will give us what we need to continue that work. He longs for us to be closer to Him, and He knows it's a struggle. After all, He made us, and He knows full well the human nature we're fighting against.

We Are Equipped

Have you ever started a big project and realized once you were in the thick of it you didn't have all of the tools you needed? It's frustrating, isn't it? When it comes to spiritual gifts, God hasn't short-changed us. We already have everything we need.

> His divine power has given us everything we need for a godly life through our knowledge of him who called us by his own glory and goodness.
>
> II Peter 1:3 (NIV)

We can live differently from the way we have been living. We can live differently from those around us. Though we are surrounded by greed and excess, we have the power to escape their pull on us. It is exceedingly challenging at times to live a godly life. But we should not forget God's promises, lest we feel overwhelmed. They can give us the motivation we need to push through the challenges.

God's Promises

The Bible is full of passages promising God's presence, His strength, and His help. With God on our team and the Holy Spirit living inside us, what else do we need? We are ready to face any challenge.

> So do not fear, for I am with you; do not be dismayed, for I am your God. I will strengthen you and help you; I will uphold you with my righteous right hand.
>
> Isaiah 41:10 (NIV)

Peace from God

God longs for us to bring each and every trouble to Him. He really does care about the details of our lives. If we're struggling to make changes in this area, we can bring our struggles to God in prayer. He longs to give us victory and peace.

> "Do not be anxious about anything, but in every situation, by prayer and petition, with thanksgiving, present your requests to God. And the peace of God, which transcends all understanding, will guard your hearts and your minds in Christ Jesus."
>
> Philippians 4:6-7 (NIV)

Ask and Receive

Think about how much parents love their children and long to give them good things. God's love for us is orders of magnitude greater than the love parents have for their children.

> Ask and it will be given to you; seek and you will find; knock and the door will be opened to you. For everyone who asks receives; the one who seeks finds; and to the one who knocks, the door will be opened. Which of you, if your son asks for bread, will give him a stone? Or if he asks for a fish, will give him a snake? If you, then, though you are evil, know how to give good gifts to your children, how much more will your Father in heaven give good gifts to those who ask him!
>
> Matthew 7:7–11 (NIV)

He doesn't give us everything we want because our wants don't always align with what's best for us. But we can believe if we are earnestly seeking to live in a way that glorifies Him, He absolutely wants to honor that request. If we're striving to use our time and possessions in a godly way, He is ready and waiting to bless our commitment.

❧ 16 ☙

Unholy Mess No More

When I have a first appointment with a new client, one of my favorite questions to ask is, "What is your main goal? If we could wave a magic wand and produce the ideal outcome, what would it look like? What would it feel like?"

What's your vision for an uncluttered home and life? You may not know exactly what it will look like and feel like as you work through this process. But I can promise you this—letting go of the clutter that's distracting you from focusing on Him will bless you in ways you can't even imagine.

Oh, how our Father loves us! He longs for His children to be close to Him. He desires it so much that He gave us the most precious gifts imaginable—the gift of His Son Jesus and the gift of His Spirit. What a tragedy it would be to miss out on intimacy with God because we chose to cling to things we don't need. Let's trust Him and cling closer to Him instead.

I can't think of a better way to close than with this passage:

> For this reason I kneel before the Father, from whom every family in heaven and on earth derives its name. I pray that out of his glorious riches he may strengthen you with power through his Spirit in your inner being, so that Christ may dwell in your hearts through faith. And I pray that you, being rooted and established in love, may have power, together with all the Lord's holy people, to grasp how wide and long and high and deep is the love of Christ, and to know this love that surpasses knowledge—that you may be filled to the measure of all the fullness of God.
>
> Now to him who is able to do immeasurably more than all we ask or imagine, according to his power that is at work within us, to him be glory in the church and in Christ Jesus throughout all generations, for ever and ever! Amen.
>
> Ephesians 3:14–21 (NIV)

This is my prayer for each one of you. I pray that God's Spirit will strengthen you in your journey. I pray that you can comprehend how vast God's love for you is so you can be filled to overflowing. And I pray that God will do more than all you could ask or imagine so you can spend the rest of your life shouting His praises.

I can't wait to hear how God blesses you. I am confident He will.

Endnotes

Chapter 1: What is Clutter?

1   Joshua Becker, *The More of Less: Finding the Life You Want Under Everything You Own*. Colorado Springs: WaterBrook Press, 2016. Kindle Edition.

Chapter 2: How Does Clutter Affect Us?

2   "Lost and Found: The Average American Spends 2.5 Days Each Year Looking for Lost Items Collectively Costing US Households $2.7 Billion Annually in Replacement Costs," *Pixie Technology Inc.,* 2 May 2017, accessed 5 June 2020. https://www.prnewswire.com/news-releases/lost-and-found-the-average-american-spends-25-days-each-year-looking-for-lost-items-collectively-costing-us-households-27-billion-annually-in-replacement-costs-300449305.html.

3   Chloie Reichel, "Cutting through the clutter: What research says about tidying up," *Journalist's* Resource, 11 February 2019, accessed 2 December 2019. https://journalistsresource.org/studies/society/housing/marie-kondo-konmari-tidying-up-research/.

4   "A Cluttered Kitchen Can Nudge Us To Overeat, Study Finds...," *National Public Radio,* 15 February 2016, accessed 25 November 2019. https://www.npr.org/sections/thesalt/2016/02/15/466567647/a-cluttered-kitchen-can-nudge-us-to-overeat-study-finds.

5   David F. Tolin, Randy O. Frost, Gail Steketee, Krista D. Gray, and Kristin E. Fitch, "The economic and social burden of compulsive hoarding," *National Center for Biotechnology Information*, 1 July 2008, accessed 25 November 2019. https://www.ncbi.nlm.nih.gov/pmc/articles/PMC3018686/.

6   Peter Walsh, "Review: Lose the Clutter, Lose the Weight," *Times Union,* 15 April 2015, accessed 25 November 2019. https://blog.timesunion.com/healthylife/review-lose-the-clutter-lose-the-weight-by-peter-walsh/16630/.

7   Michael Blanding, "Psychology: Your Attention, Please," *Princeton Alumni Weekly*, 3 June 2015, accessed 2 December 2019. https://paw.princeton.edu/article/psychology-your-attention-please.

8   Catherine A. Roster, Joseph R. Ferrari, and M. Peter Jurkat, "The dark side of home: Assessing possession 'clutter' on subjective well-being," *Science Direct*, June 2016, accessed 2 Dec. 2019. https://doi.org/10.1016/j.jenvp.2016.03.003.

9   Sara R. Jaffee, Ken B. Hanscombe, Clair M. A. Haworth, Oliver S. P. Davis, Robert Plomin, "Chaotic Homes and Children's Disruptive Behavior: A Longitudinal Cross-Lagged Twin Study," 30 April 2012, Accessed 2 December 2019. https://doi.org/10.1177/0956797611431693.

10   "Falls Prevention Facts," *National Council on Aging*, accessed 25 November 2019. https://www.ncoa.org/news/resources-for-reporters/get-the-facts/falls-prevention-facts/.

11   "The Fire Safety Dangers of Having Too Much 'Stuff' in the Workplace and in the Home," *National Institutes of Health: Office Management*, accessed 25 November 2019. https://www.ors.od.nih.gov/News/Pages/The-Fire-Safety-Dangers-of-Having-Too-Much-'Stuff'-in-the-Workplace-and-in-the-Home.aspx.

Chapter 3: What's My Clutter Story?

12   Lucy Maud Montgomery, *Anne of Green Gables*. Project Gutenberg, see esp. chap. 38, "The Bend in the road" accessed 2 December 2019. https://www.cs.cmu.edu/~rgs/anne-table.html.

13   Deyan G.,"45 Scary Smartphone Addiction Statistics for 2019," *TechJury,* 18 March 2019, accessed 13 December 2019. https://techjury.net/stats-about/smartphone-addiction/.

14   Kevin Jackson, "A brief history of the smartphone," *Science Node,* 25 July 2018, accessed 13 Dec. 2019. https://sciencenode.org/feature/How%20did%20smartpho nes%20evolve.php.

Chapter 7: Godly Priorities

15   John Piper, "Free from Money, Rich Toward God," *Desiring God,* 4 January 2016, accessed 18 Dec. 2019. https://www.desiringgod.org/messages/free-from-money-rich-toward-god.

16   "Matthew Henry's Commentary —Verses 24-28," *Bible Gateway,* accessed 18 December 2019. https://www.biblegateway.com/resources/matthew-henry/Matt.16.24-Matt.16.28.

17   Luke Timothy Johnson, *Sharing Possessions: What Faith Demands*, Second Edition, Kindle Edition, Loc 713-722.

Chapter 8: God's Promises

18   *Ciudad de Angeles,* accessed 18 December 2019. https://www.ciudaddeangeles.org.

19   *Mission Upreach,* accessed 18 December 2019. https://missionupreach.org.

Chapter 10: What is the Overall Organizing Process?

20   Emily P. Freeman, "21: Find A No Mentor," *Emily P. Freeman,* accessed 27 July 2020. https://emilypfreeman.com/podcast/the-next-right-thing/21.

Chapter 11: How Do I Declutter My Schedule and My Mind?

21   Trevor Atwood, "The King's Clock: How The Sabbath Shapes Our Time and Money," *City Church*, 05 May 2019, accessed 13 Dec. 2019. https://www.borocitychurch.com/sermon/the-kings-clock-how-the-sabbath-shapes-our-time-and-money/.

22   "FOMO," *Farlex Dictionary of Idioms*, 2015. Farlex, Inc., accessed 13 December 2019. https://idioms.thefreedictionary.com/FOMO.

Chapter 12: How Do I Declutter My Belongings?

23   Margareta Magnusson, *The Gentle Art of Swedish Death Cleaning: How to Free Yourself and Your Family from a Lifetime of Clutter*. Scribner. Kindle Edition, p. 1.

24   Ibid. p. 9.

25   Kevin Kruse, "The 80/20 Rule And How It Can Change Your Life," *Forbes*, 7 March 2016, accessed 20 December 2019. https://www.forbes.com/sites/kevinkruse/2016/03/07/80-20-rule/.

26   Marie Kondō, *The Life-Changing Magic of Tidying Up: The Japanese Art of Decluttering and Organizing*, accessed 22 April 2020. https://www.amazon.com/Life-Changing-Magic-Tidying-Decluttering-Organizing/dp/1607747308.

27   Dana White, "OOOoooh, "Contain"er . . . Now I Get It!," *A Slob Comes Clean*, 21 May 2010, accessed 20 December 2019. https://www.aslobcomesclean.com/2010/05/ooooooh-container-now-i-get-it/.

28   "Contain," *American Heritage® Dictionary of the English Language*, Fifth Edition. S.v., accessed 20 December 2019. https://www.thefreedictionary.com/contain.

Chapter 13: What are the Obstacles to Letting Go?

29 Joshua Fields Millburn and Ryan Nicodemus, "Getting Rid of Just-in-Case Items: 20 Dollars, 20 Minutes," *The Minimalists*, accessed 26 December 2019. https://www.theminimalists.com/jic/.

30 "Emotional Strategies for Decluttering (part 2)," *HeartWork Organizing,* 15 February 2015, accessed 26 December 2019. https://heartworkorg.com/2015/02/15/emotional-strategies-for-decluttering-part-2/.

Chapter 14: How Do I Prevent Future Clutter?

31 "How To REALLY Buy Less "Stuff" We Do Not Need," *Honestly Modern*, accessed 27 December 2019. https://www.honestlymodern.com/how-to-really-buy-less-stuff-we-do-not-need/.

32 James Clear, *Atomic Habits: An Easy & Proven Way to Build Good Habits & Break Bad Ones*. New York: Avery, 2018. Kindle Edition.

33 Gretchen Rubin, *The Four Tendencies*. New York: Harmony Books, 2017. Kindle Edition, p. 6.

Acknowledgement

To Stephanie McClellan, my first editor at the Kingsport Times News: Late in 2016, I walked into your office to boldly request the opportunity to write a regular organizing column. It was an awkward conversation to be sure. Thanks for taking a chance on me. Without the experience I have had writing that column, I don't think I would ever have written a book.

To Holly Nelms Viers at the Kingsport Times News: Thank you for introducing me and my company to Times News readers before I began writing my column and for introducing my book when it was published.

To Carol Broyles, my current editor at the Kingsport Times News: Thanks for helping me with my column each month. It's a pleasure to work with you!

To Heather Cook: Thank you for your advice and encouragement as a first-time author. I learned so much from seeing how you navigated this challenge and how you've used your book to further your business goals.

To Teresa Inghram: Thank you for speaking God's Word so powerfully in a Bible study years ago so that I could not only be blessed and challenged by it over the years but could also pass it along to others for their inspiration. I'm so glad that God brought our paths together and that we could reconnect for the purpose of this book. Isn't it amazing how in God's kingdom, we are forever sisters no matter how much time has passed?

To Donna Waldron: Thank you for being a living and breathing example of faith in my life. You and Phil have allowed God to use you in such powerful ways to bless people all over the world. Many orphaned and abandoned children found a home because you said "yes" to God's calling to establish Ciudad de Angeles. Many people of all ages in Honduras have had their physical and spiritual needs met because you said "yes" to God's calling to minister in Honduras by establishing Mission Upreach. You continue to say "yes" to God, even when the path is unclear and your own provision in doubt. And God continues to reward your faithfulness and to bless more and more people because of it. You inspire me to do the same.

To Audra Steadman: Thank you so much for using your gift for photography to help create my book cover. Thank you also for the photographs you've created for some of my newspaper articles. You have so much talent, and I can't wait to see how God will use your gifts to glorify Him.

To Jenny Kontos and the staff at Hillhouse Creative: I had an idea for how I wanted this book cover to look, but I had no clue how to make that idea come together. It was a difficult balance between a design that would suggest clutter but would also catch a potential reader's eye and draw them in. Thank you for going the extra mile to create a cover that I could be proud of and that so perfectly represented my vision.

To the Faithful Organizers group: I love connecting during our devotionals at NAPO conferences and with virtual devotionals and webinars. You have helped me realize that the work we do with our clients is a ministry. What a gift to be a part of this group of organizers who are also sisters in Christ!

To my clients: Thank you for the trust you have placed in me to help you organize. It is such a joy to work alongside each of you! The time we spend together sorting through belongings, discussing the best way to arrange items in your home, or just talking about our lives are highlights of my week. Whether you know it or not, I learn something valuable from each one of you. I am so grateful that God has allowed our paths to cross.

To Pam Johnson: Thanks for being my writing buddy! We've worked on writing projects in a condo at the beach and in a cabin in the woods. You've given me great advice and encouraged me when I was overwhelmed. I'm so grateful for your friendship!

To Laurie Harvey: Thanks for being my sidekick and business partner. It has been wonderful to have a friend to walk alongside me in our business. Your encouragement means the world to me, and I am so grateful for your friendship.

To Shawndra Holmberg: I could never have found someone more perfectly suited to help me create and launch this book. When I initially contacted you, I wasn't even sure I had the ability to do this or that my writing was worth being shared. You have given me the courage to believe that God gave me this message so that I could share it, and you've shown me exactly how to do that. Hold Your Hand (HYH) Book Coach is aptly named, as you have literally done that for me each step of the way! Thanks for everything you've done to turn my dream into a reality. I am forever grateful and can't wait to do it all again in a future book.

To my parents and my family: You have been beside me every step of the way in creating this business and in writing this book. You've always given me the encouragement and support I needed at each stage. You've listened to me cry and complain, and you've celebrated the small victories. Each one of you has believed in me when I didn't even believe in myself. You'll never be able to understand how much that has meant to me. I am blessed beyond measure to have you in my life.

To Emma, my firstborn daughter and the first real writer in the family: I am so thankful for your encouragement during this process. Though our writing genres couldn't be more different, you understand the ins and outs of the process and have given me such useful insight. I am so inspired by your intelligence, your creativity, and your mastery of words. You've been independent from such an early age. I still admire you for heading to Malibu, California for your first year of college and to London for your second year. Although we don't get to see each other nearly as often as I'd like because of our distance apart, I treasure every text, phone call, FaceTime or Zoom call, and every visit. I love you and am so proud of you!

To Lydia, my youngest daughter: I'm so glad you moved closer so that we could spend more time together. I'm honored that you prioritize spending time with me.

Thank you so much for the encouragement you give me in my writing and in my business. You've got such a big heart for people and so much creativity. I can't wait to see all of the ways that you will use your passion and personality to bless others as you have blessed me. I love you and am so proud of you!

To my husband, Eric: How can I even begin to thank you enough for all of the ways you have contributed to my organizing business and to this book? I am 100% convinced that I would never have even started an organizing business if not for you. I talked about it for years, did lots of research, talked to several organizers, got advice from many friends and family members, but I just couldn't bring myself to make that giant leap. Finally, on the Silver Comet bicycle trail in Georgia, you said the exact words I needed to hear to finally believe that I could do it. But more than that, you promised to support me every step of the way and to help me in any way that you could. And you have certainly held true to your promise. You never seem to tire of me asking for your opinion, venting my frustrations, or just talking about the details of a big organizing project. Writing this book has occupied so much of my time, energy, and focus for the past year, and you've been more patient and supportive than I could imagine. You truly are God's greatest gift on this earth to me. After thirty-six years together, you're still the one. And you always will be.

To my Heavenly Father: God, You are so good to me. Everything I have is Yours. I am humbled that You could use me. My deepest desire is to praise and glorify you with all that You've given me. I just want to point everyone to You, God, for You alone are worthy of praise.

୫ ୦ଃ

About the Author

A ngie Hyche has worked as a professional organizer and the owner of Shipshape Solutions in Kingsport, Tennessee since 2016. She provides custom organizing services, helping her clients create functional and inviting spaces in their homes and offices. She is a Certified Professional Organizer® (CPO®). She is an active member of the National Association of Productivity and Organizing Professionals (NAPO) and Faithful Organizers, and is a frequent speaker for group presentations on organizing, time management, and the spiritual implications of clutter. She writes a monthly organizing column for her local newspaper and gives monthly organizing demonstrations for a local TV talk show. When she's not organizing, Angie loves to hike and ride on bicycle trails with her husband Eric, to spend time with her two daughters Emma and Lydia, and to act in community theatre productions. You can find more information about her business at her website https://shipshape.solutions, and sign up for her monthly organizing tips. She would love readers to share their wins, challenges, thoughts, and blessings with her through email (angie@shipshape.solutions).

If you found this book useful, consider leaving a review. It helps others find this book.